The 800-Pound Gorilla of Sales

The 800-Pound Gorilla of Sales

How to Dominate Your Market

Bill Guertin

WILEY

John Wiley & Sons, Inc.

Published by John Wiley & Sons, Inc., Hoboken, New Jersey.
Published simultaneously in Canada.

For general information on our other products and services or for technical support,
please contact our Customer Care Department within the United States at (800)
762-2974, outside the United States at (317) 572-3993 or fax (317) 572-4002.

Wiley also publishes its books in a variety of electronic formats. Some content that
appears in print may not be available in electronic books. For more information about
Wiley products, visit our web site at www.wiley.com.

Library of Congress Cataloging-in-Publication Data:

Guertin, Bill.
    The 800-pound gorilla of sales : how to dominate your market / by Bill Guertin.
        p. cm.
    Includes bibliographical references.
    ISBN 978-0-470-49675-6 (cloth)
    1. Selling. 2. Selling—Case studies. 3. Success in business.
    I. Title. II. Title: Eight hundred pound gorilla of sales.
    HF5438.25.G84 2010
    658.85—dc22

                                                            2009021648

Printed in the United States of America.

10 9 8 7 6 5 4 3 2 1

To my incredible wife, Sherri,
and our three children, Kyle, Ryan, and Tyler,
my inspirations and my true loves,
who constantly remind me
that being a husband and father
is the greatest profession in life. . .
and to my parents,
Ronald and Barbara Guertin,
who taught me that in the first place.

CONTENTS

PREFACE

During my journey of writing this book, something happened to me that was very humbling: I met dozens of very talented, very successful salespeople who are doing things *way* differently than I would do them myself.

And that's a very good thing.

First, I needed to be exposed to new ways of doing things myself. When you're a professional of any kind, there's a real danger in becoming locked into the way you do things without exposing yourself to other tactics and techniques. During the many hours of writing, research, and interviewing, I was continually humbled by the depth of talent and generosity that exists in today's professional selling world. I'm deeply grateful to everyone who contributed to this work. It's truly a collaboration of many.

Second, on occasion, many of us get a case of inflated human ego that holds us back from becoming what we were truly meant to be. We think we know it all, and so we stop learning; there's no reason to go looking for new answers, because we've got enough of them to succeed. Every now and then, we need someone to knock us off our perch and make us look around at what the rest of the world is doing.

Thinking you know it all is the first step toward extinction. I'm grateful to those whose contributions here allowed me to see that firsthand.

Third, as I have been inspired by each of these contributors, my ultimate intent for you, the reader, is to use these words and thoughts as a springboard for you to go above and beyond what each of these contributors have achieved. You're going to have ideas for your own career pop into your head as you read each chapter. Have a pencil and paper ready. I believe in the use of information as inspiration, and you will ultimately gain so much more from your time spent reading if you capture your inspired thoughts at the moment of conception.

Finally, I want to thank you for being a reader of my work. I'm truly humbled by others who have found value enough in the work that I do to invest their time and money into it. Thanks for allowing me to be a part of your life journey.

Your thoughts and comments are always welcome; please feel free to contact me at bill@The800PoundGorilla .com. There are other articles and resources available to you via my web site, www.The 800PoundGorilla.com. I'd love to hear from you regarding your personal experiences, revelations, and insights for potential future editions, articles, and examples of *The 800-Pound Gorilla of Sales*.

Rock on!

ACKNOWLEDGMENTS

A heartfelt thank-you:

To my wife, Sherri, for her support throughout this project and for her patience in being a "writer's widow" for a good part of the winter of 2009.

To Matt Holt, Lauren Lynch, and Christine Moore of John Wiley & Sons, all true professionals who saw something in me that I didn't even see myself.

To Arthur Chou of WBusiness Books, for your friendship and all that you've risked on my behalf, and for the freedom to pursue this project.

To all those who took time out of their busy schedules to share their wisdom and discuss their passion for selling with me, many of whom I was not able to include in this volume because of space limitations.

To my *Reality Sells* writing partner and great friend Andrew Corbus, whose feedback and ideas always seem to generate something great (everyone who writes should have an Andy Corbus in their life).

And to God Almighty, who constantly reminds me of who's in control.

PROLOGUE
AWAKENING — DAY ONE

Rain.

"Could it possibly be any uglier for my first day on the job?" Adam grumbled to himself, looking out the kitchen window and up to the gray sky with a coffee cup in his hand. The all-night downpour had brief, violent periods of thunder and lightning, and now in the early morning gloom had diminished to a light, steady sprinkle, just enough to keep the pavement soaked. As much as he might need one, Adam decided not to take an umbrella; he wanted to make a good first impression on his first day, and the thought of carrying a big umbrella into his new office sounded too geeky to him.

He jogged to his car in the apartment building's parking space, using his new briefcase as a shield on top of his head, poured himself inside, and shook everything off as he got settled. It was a 25-minute commute on a good day; and this was *not* going to be a good day for traffic.

It still felt good, no matter what the weather, Adam thought. He was excited about living in Chicago. The apartment in Rogers Park was a lucky find, and the move from the suburbs was something he had looked forward to ever since he graduated from college a year ago. The furniture sales job in his home town was just something to hold him over until he could find that first real job in the big city, and here he was, driving to work to Chicago. Chi-*caw*-go. City of the Big Shoulders. The Town That Billy Sunday Couldn't Shut Down. Wasn't Billy Sunday a former Chicago cop? Something to do with Dillinger, he seemed to remember.

No matter. He turned left onto Halsted and flipped on his satellite radio, looking for something to interest him. The sports station was reading scores he'd already known from the night before, and his favorite music station had a song he particularly disliked. His third choice was the *Wall Street Journal* radio channel, which he listened to often. It was an interview of some type.

"...but there's a recession on, and people are pulling back everywhere. Don't you think that salespeople all over the world feel especially vulnerable right now?" one voice asked.

"Vulnerable? Sure," said an older, more reassuring voice. "If you only focus on what you sell and how much you sell it for, you *are* vulnerable, because your product and your price is all you have. If you focus on those things which make *dominant* companies successful, however, it's much easier to survive. Not *easy* to survive, mind you, just easier."

Hmm, Adam thought to himself, pouting out his lower lip as he drove. I wonder what he's talking about?

"Whether the markets are up or down, there will still be all kinds of phenomenal breakthroughs in products and services produced over the next 10 years. But if you don't have someone who can champion them, they'll never make it to the mainstream. That's why our salespeople are so important today. Products alone can't change lives; people have to drive that change. The 800-Pound Gorillas—the dominant players in the market—will be the ones to make it happen. And the companies and individuals that can do that will be in demand no matter what the economy is doing."

Who is this guy? Adam thought.

"Our company has identified 12 attributes shared by all 800-Pound Gorillas—the dominant companies or individuals in a marketplace that get more than their fair share," Mystery Guest said. "As a salesperson or a company, if you can master a majority of them, you'll be unstoppable."

"Twelve attributes," repeated the interviewer slowly, as if thinking what they might be. "And just what are those 12 things?"

"That's for us at Consolidated to know," the guest smiled. "And for our customers to experience firsthand."

"Consolidated?" Adam said out loud, looking down at the radio. "That's *my* new company!"

"That's too bad," chuckled the interviewer, "Are you hiring?"

"Not anymore," Mystery Guest said with a smile. His voice seemed to carry through the radio and rest on Adam's shoulder. Was he talking to *me?* Adam wondered.

"Our guest has been Peter Strahan, CEO of Consolidated Universal. Thanks so much, Peter, for joining us this morning on *Wall Street Journal* Radio." A music bed played, and another announcer came on to promote the next segment, but Adam didn't hear any of it.

How about that, Adam thought. *Peter Strahan on the radio.* He chuckled. "What are the odds of me catching *that* on my first day?" he asked aloud. He began to wonder if part of his training session would include the 12 things. *What did he call them? Attributes?* If it was important, he was sure he'd learn them soon.

He pulled into the parking lot according to his instructions from the HR department. A smiling elderly gentleman addressed him from inside the tiny parking attendant's box.

"So," he said with a smile. "You must be Adam. Heather from HR told me to be expectin' you. Your first day, right?"

"Yes, sir," said Adam, smiling a bit nervously.

"That's excitin' for you. Congratulations. Yo' gonna love it. I'm Julius; you'll see me every day here in this box, Lord willin'. Let me know how things go f'ya today."

"Okay, Julius, I'll do that." The yellow stop arm lifted in front of Adam's car, and he smiled as he pulled in. If everyone was like Julius, he would feel at home right away.

Adam walked tentatively into his training class. Several people were already there, including a few that were older than he had expected and many with Consolidated badges indicating they'd been there for a long time. He stopped in the doorway, thinking he had chosen the wrong room.

"No, this is it; you're in the right place," a woman near the door said sweetly. Adam followed the voice with his eyes to find a sharply dressed woman in her 30s in the second row of seats. There were maybe 25 chairs in the room, and all that were left were the half-dozen near the front. Adam chose one of them, and quickly sat down. Several people were engaged in subdued conversation with each other, while others seemed to expect him and were staring him down.

"Welcome!" he heard in a half-whisper from behind him. "You must be Adam."

Feeling obligated to turn around, Adam gave a quick glance around to the others, several of whom seemed to be looking straight at him and smiling. *Nothing like intimidating the new guy on his first day,* he thought to himself. He looked around sheepishly, nodding his head at everyone. "And you?" he asked the woman, extending his hand.

"I'm Belinda," she said. "I'm in sales, too. It's good to meet you. You're going to love it today!" she gushed.

"Well, I'm not sure what to ex—" Adam's sentence was cut off by the entrance of an impeccably dressed gentleman with graying hair and a neatly trimmed goatee. Everyone in the room obviously knew who he was. Everyone except Adam.

"Good morning, everyone!" the gentleman boomed enthusiastically.

"Good morning, Mr. Strahan!" everyone behind Adam chanted in unison. The conversations stopped immediately.

Strahan! Adam thought to himself. *Peter Strahan? The guy on the radio this morning?* He knew that voice had sounded familiar.

"It's a great day to be alive, isn't it?" he asked, and the group nodded their heads in agreement.

"It's a great day for me because I get to be here for all of you on behalf of our newest account executive." Peter then looked directly at Adam, smiling. "Let's all welcome Adam Perry to the sales team." Applause broke out behind him as Adam turned shyly toward the group to accept the welcome.

"I've read up on Adam, and from what I hear in HR and from the others you've interviewed with here, Adam, I know you'll be a valuable addition to the company." His voice sounded so sincere, so trusting and genuine, Adam thought.

"Just to bring you up to speed, Adam, the first part of the orientation that each employee receives here at Consolidated is from me, and anyone from our Leadership Team is invited to attend if they like. As often as I travel, I don't get to see many of them as often as I used to, so you see there are a few who have come to hear me do my 30 minutes."

Okay, that explains a lot, Adam smiled to himself.

"What I'm going to be doing today is introducing you to our '12 Attributes' and how we use them here at Consolidated as the foundation for maintaining and growing our position as the number one provider in our industry. Since we have very little turnover, we don't have these get-togethers as often as we used to; so Adam, I hope you don't mind a little company for the first part of your orientation today."

"Not at all, sir," Adam replied, a little louder than he had intended.

And so, Peter began to speak.

Wouldn't you just love to know what Peter was about to say?

The good news is that after you've read this book—*you'll be able to give that speech.*

Who do you relate to in the story so far? Are you a Peter Strahan, leader of a team that's looking for leadership? Are you one of those salespeople in the meeting who's craving inspiration, new ideas, and new ways to generate the kind of income you know you're capable of earning? Perhaps you're Adam, just starting out and wanting to know how to get to the top in the most efficient way possible.

Wherever you are on your sales career journey, this book will help you to achieve more of what you want.

In every industry, in every competitive category, there are companies and individuals that just seem to *win* more often. They are, as the business media calls them, the "800-Pound Gorillas": the dominant players, the ones others emulate, and the ones who are constantly being watched, analyzed, and admired.

As a successful salesperson, entrepreneur, and speaker, I've studied and interviewed hundreds of companies and individuals about what they did to propel themselves to the top of the mountain. From each interview and study, there was one or more of a dozen attributes that seemed to come up over and over again in each of the dominant players. Collectively, these attributes are:

1. Thinking Bigger Than Anyone Else
2. Being Authentic
3. Rattling the Cage
4. Doing What Others Won't
5. Being a Hero to Those You Serve
6. Talking Less and Doing More
7. Adding Value
8. Being the One Others Quote
9. Getting Beyond Rejection
10. Knowing the Competition
11. Being Passionate
12. Mastering the Fundamentals

No one company or individual possesses them all, but the best practice a majority of them.

This is not an all-inclusive list; in fact, an argument could be made for the inclusion of any of a dozen additional characteristics of 800-Pound Gorillas. What you'll learn in the context of this book, however, is that if you go after becoming the dominant player using these 12 attributes, any others you might include will form naturally as a result.

Dive in with an open mind, a pencil, and a notepad. The ideas that spring from your reading will be the most valuable resource you'll receive.

INTRODUCTION:
WHY IT'S GOOD TO BE AN
800-POUND GORILLA

You've seen them on *Animal Planet*, in their habitat at the zoo, or on the cover of *National Geographic*. Sometimes graying; sometimes fatter than you'd like them to be but always fascinating, the African lowland gorilla is a creature that we're intrigued by because of its resemblance to us.

Is that really what we look like? We ask ourselves as we watch them pick nits from their fur, scratch their rear ends, and fall on top of each other. They're interesting to us because they give us a glimpse into what we would be like if we weren't—well, if we weren't domesticated.

The male adult lowland gorilla normally weighs in at anywhere from 300 to 450 pounds, but a few have been known to grow larger. The largest gorilla on record was a male who weighed in at 638 pounds and lived at the San Diego Zoo during the 1930s and 40s. There has been no gorilla on record that has ever officially weighed in any larger than that, but the intimidating picture of an 800-pound gorilla has fascinated the business media for decades.

The first use of the term is difficult to trace, but as early as the 1960s, the term "800-Pound Gorilla" was used to describe the big oil companies, automobile companies, and manufacturing giants of the day. They're the biggest of the big, the headlines said, because of their sheer size and influence; they set the rules and pave the way for how the rest of us do business, whether we like it or not.

Today, we might consider companies like Microsoft, McDonald's, Wal-Mart, or Google examples of 800-Pound Gorillas. When they do something or make a change, it affects many other people who are often forced to make changes themselves because of their competitive relationship to the company. If McDonald's changes its menu, it's big news, and competitors scramble to see how they should respond. When Microsoft changes its operating software, others that have built products on the Microsoft platform must conform them to the new platform.

Individuals can also be categorized as 800-Pound Gorillas. Talk show host Oprah Winfrey can make a book into a best-seller with a simple endorsement. Billionaire developer Donald Trump can put his brand on a project and turn it into a moneymaker. Well-known investor Warren Buffett is watched closely by many of the smartest minds in the financial world. Any of these people could easily be called 800-Pound Gorillas because of the influence they carry in their fields.

The descriptor has become so much a part of our culture that the Merriam-Webster Online Dictionary now contains a definition of 800-Pound Gorilla: "one that is dominating or uncontrollable because of great size or power."

Translation: It's good to be an 800-Pound Gorilla.

As a salesperson, you've known this all along. There are probably others in your company or industry who sell a lot more than you do right now. They're the ones who sit at the head table at the annual sales conference and accept the big awards. They're the ones you hear about during a meeting with a potential client who says "we're already working with someone right now." They're the ones who always seem to be a step ahead and a leg up.

As an account rep, sales manager, and general manager for several small-market radio stations for more than 25 years, I learned firsthand what worked for business owners—and what didn't. I've put together, sold, and implemented hundreds of media plans, marketing programs, and commercial campaigns. And I've learned that when it comes to sales, you don't have to be the biggest one in the jungle to command 800-Pound Gorilla status with customers and suppliers.

I took the expertise that I've developed in media and created an independent sales training company that specializes in assisting professional sports teams' ticket sales departments. In working for many of the most successful sports franchises in the world, I've seen from the inside what makes their organizations the 800-Pound Gorillas of their sport— whether it be the National Basketball Association, the National Football League, the National Hockey League, Major League Baseball, Major League Soccer, or any of the dozens of minor league sports organizations throughout the country.

The 800-Pound Gorillas of Sales are individuals and companies that do things more successfully than their peers, and who enjoy sales results that are far superior to the industry average. Throughout the pages of this book, you'll learn how they do it, what they did to get there, and how you might incorporate what they're doing into your own system of doing business. You'll hear their stories, failures, and triumphs; and you'll learn what you can do to become the dominant player in your own business category.

If you play your cards right, soon you'll be the one who others watch, admire, and attempt to emulate.

Look out, world; here you come!

LIVE LARGE, TAKE CHARGE

Why 800-Pound Gorillas Think Bigger Than Anyone Else

It's five years from today. Five years into the future.

On that morning five years from now, you'll wake up with the help of an ear implant that doesn't disturb anyone else; take a shower with an antiterrorist body wash that wards off microbes of mass destruction; get into your 100 percent electric, nonpolluting car; and pull into your office or workplace drinking coffee from a reusable cup that knows how many times you've reused it and credits you automatically at the convenience mart the next time you stop in.

Pretty cool, eh?

What's happened in the future is that the 800-Pound Gorillas of the world have taken action to make these new products successful. They were the companies that created the innovations, saw the market potential, and did what needed to be done to bring them to life. They were the salespeople in those companies who took the products, identified the markets, created the sales plans, and went out and made it happen. By their efforts, they made our lives a little easier, our planet a little more livable; and they made a few dollars doing it.

Will you be one of them?

By our definition, 800-Pound Gorillas are the dominant players in any marketplace whose tactics and techniques result in an "unfair share" of the available business. They're the trendsetters, the ones others watch and follow. From technological toys to colon-cleaning products, they are the movers and shakers in every major business category whose efforts are inspiring others, helping others to take action, and setting the pace for everyone else to follow.

The saying goes that nothing happens until somebody sells something. That's only partially true. The reality is that nothing *truly* happens until an 800-Pound Gorilla gets hold of it.

Imagine that Google had entered the online search business thinking that it only had enough guts to build a modest platform; that Ticketmaster was content to be a regional box office; or that the New York Yankees had resigned themselves to being just another baseball team. Instead, each has become an icon of its genre—a presence that's impossible to ignore as a competitor.

Before we go any further, let's be clear about the term we're using throughout this journey. Some would argue that the term 800-Pound Gorilla is synonymous with aggression, bullying, or disregard for ethics or decorum. Others may even have the image of King Kong swatting away the competition from atop the Empire State Building. Interestingly, for the majority of the people you're about to meet, that image couldn't be further from the truth. Becoming a dominant player often happens not because of one's brute strength, but because of the things one does to earn his position through strategic planning, conscious choices, relentless execution, and/or good old-fashioned hard work. If such an individual's results give others the impression of a King Kong-like competitor, well, that may be purely a case of mistaken identity.

Selling is a risky business. There is a leap of faith that's necessary when choosing to invest time and energy in a job, a company, or an industry when the eventual payoff lies somewhere down the road. One of the key differences between those who plod along and those who become 800-Pound Gorillas is the latter's ability to think bigger—or take bigger risks—than anyone else.

> Those who have become the dominant players in their chosen fields have already asked and answered a few fundamental questions that suggest they are thinking bigger than others:
>
> Where do I stand now in comparison to others?
> Where is the future of my industry, and what will I need to do to be a part of it?
> Do I want to be the dominant player and enjoy all the benefits that go along with it?
> How must I think—and what am I willing to risk—in order to get there?

New York Yankees owner and former day-to-day operations chief George Steinbrenner is one of the biggest thinkers in all of professional sports. He has been known for taking huge risks on the best players and paying them record-breaking salaries—and over the years, his team has become one of the dominant franchises in the sport. To say the least, Steinbrenner is driven to succeed. "Winning is the most important thing in my life after breathing. Breathing first, winning next," said Steinbrenner, when discussing how he ran the Yankees. Although he passed control of the team to his son Hal in November 2008, the Yankees are easily the most valuable baseball franchise on the planet today: *Forbes* magazine estimated its market value in 2008 at approximately $1.3 billion, far higher than the number two franchise, the cross-town New York Mets, valued at $824 million; and the Yankees' archrivals, the Boston Red Sox, at $816 million. By every measure, the Yankees are in a class by themselves, and baseball fans are passionate about the Yankees in one of two ways: they either love them or they hate them.

Since the team's inception more than a century ago, the Yankees have won more World Series championships (26), have more representatives in the Baseball Hall of Fame (23), and have had the highest average home attendance (42,785 in 2008) of any team in baseball. Although every team sees a challenge when Derek Jeter, Alex Rodriguez, Mark Teixeira, Jorge Posada, CC Sabathia, and the other Yankees come to town, the teams' owners love what the Yankees do to increase the excitement level—and fan attendance—in their ballparks; their average visiting attendance (34,477 in 2008) is the highest in the league.

That kind of excitement and attendance comes from big thinking; and it also comes at a price. Steinbrenner's

2008 player payroll was $209 million, a full 30 percent higher than any other team in baseball. New Yankee Stadium—a brand-new ballpark built directly across the street from the original 1923 Yankee Stadium—opened in 2009 at a cost of $1.6 billion. And although the Yankees organization touts the fact that 85 percent of the seats are less than $100, its average per-game ticket price is the most expensive in all of sports.

Steinbrenner hates to lose; which is why he and his Yankees will continue to be the 800-Pound Gorilla of professional baseball in the United States.

So is that all it takes to become a dominant player? Get a big pile of money, buy the best players, and put it all on the line? Sometimes. Interestingly, what business is learning is that even the little guys can become 800-Pound Gorillas by *thinking* bigger than others.

The Tampa Bay Rays had a 2008 payroll of a paltry $43 million, second from the bottom in Major League Baseball. Yet, the overachieving Rays beat the Yankees and everyone else in the American League to make it to the World Series in 2008, leaving the Yankees, Boston Red Sox, Chicago White Sox, and other well-heeled clubs to sit at home and watch.

How did they do it?

In the 2007-08 off-season, Rays owner Stuart Sternberg knew he needed a clean break from the past. The team had never won more than 70 games in any of its previous 162-game seasons, and the Rays were dead last in 2007. So Sternberg began by changing the team's logo and colors, dropping the word "Devil" from the team's name (formerly the Tampa Bay Devil Rays). "We were tied to the past, and the past wasn't something we necessarily wanted to be known for," Sternberg was quoted as saying just as the team started its '08 season. "Nobody's running from it or hiding from it, and we're proud of certain aspects of it; but this is something the organization was able to really put their arms around."

Sternberg's young general manager was Andrew Friedman, a 31-year-old former Wall Street analyst who had never worked in Major League Baseball before. Using his analytical skills, Friedman saw an opportunity to put together a young, hungry group of talented players who would perform beyond others' expectations.

The team's manager was Joe Maddon, a brilliant baseball tactician and motivational guru who inspired the young players to achieve at a higher level. The result: a 97-win season, a 28 percent increase in attendance, a 99 percent jump in TV ratings, and an exciting and unexpected World Series appearance. Although they eventually lost the series to Ryan Howard and the powerful Philadelphia Phillies, the Rays' meteoric rise from worst to first was largely due to thinking bigger than anyone else had dared to think.

It's a comforting and energizing thought for everyone who has ever felt like their time will never come.

IF YOU DON'T SEE IT, CREATE IT

As noted, 800-Pound Gorillas think bigger than the average salesperson, which often means that if you discover that something doesn't exist, you look to create it yourself.

Lee Salz is a sales and management authority, author, speaker, and president of Business Expert Webinars (BEW), an e-learning company providing online webinars for businesses and individuals (www.BusinessExpertWebinars .com). Webinars are a hybrid of Web-based content and teleseminar, in which participants listen to live audio of the presenter via a phone line while viewing a PowerPoint slide show online on their computers. In October of 2007, Salz was asked to deliver a webinar to a live virtual audience of 1,300 people. The sponsor of the program had paid $25,000 for the privilege of the webinar exposure, but Salz was paid nothing for the event. "It didn't take me long to figure out that I should be doing these and getting paid," Salz says.

After the webinar, he looked for a company that would help him to deliver similar webinars to the salespeople and managers who could benefit. "I just didn't want to mess around with all the other behind-the-scenes stuff—the credit card fulfillment, the reminders to the participants, the phone lines, and all the rest."

In his search for a place in which to do that, however, Salz was astonished to find that such an animal did not exist. "No one was doing what I wanted to do," he says. "I was blown away."

So rather than be discouraged, he saw a business opportunity.

Salz began to look into ways to build a business to give speakers like himself a platform to present cutting-edge material inexpensively while allowing consumers of the information to attend for a fraction of the cost of a conference or live in-person event. He found the right technology partners, contacted fellow speakers with good content, and devised a generous revenue sharing arrangement: Put on your own webinar for $99 and host it at BEW; you'll receive a good portion of the revenue, and BEW will pick up all the other expenses and technical headaches.

"We learned a lot in those first few months," recalls Salz, "and so did our speakers."

When a webinar was scheduled, Salz would post a speaker's topic and description information. "In reading these descriptions, we learned that many were brilliant speakers on their individual topics but were not the best marketers and sellers of themselves." Their descriptions lacked sizzle, and attendance at the first webinars was weak.

"As a writer and a speaker myself, I just assumed that everyone could write a good, accurate description of their own webinars that would entice people to sign up," remembers Salz. "I found out that for most people, it's not easy to write accurately about themselves." Salz saw opportunity in the problem, and created an arm of BEW that would offer marketing and copywriting services for speakers who wanted to improve their webinar attendance and results.

Salz also learned that most speakers were "solopreneurs," often multitasking on several projects at a time. "People would call us with just a few days to go, not having sent out any e-mail invitations or promotional pieces about their upcoming webinar. We knew it wasn't because they didn't want to do a good job; they're just busy people, and needed a system of reminders to keep them on track and focused." He created a 30-day webinar coaching tool that sent e-mail prompts to each webinar presenter every few days, reminding him or her to do certain things necessary to ensure the event's success.

Business Expert Webinars now has over 150 different speakers, with 750 individual live webinars on its schedule today, and more to come.

THE ONLY PERSON YOU WON'T SURPRISE IS YOURSELF

Those who successfully think bigger are often so good at it that they don't even consider the consequences of failure. They see the finished picture so clearly—it's actually more of a surprise to them if it *doesn't* happen the way they envision it.

Louis Lautman is the executive producer of *The YES Movie*, a feature-length inspirational film released in 2009 documenting the 'how-to's' of success from more than two dozen young American millionaires (www.TheYes Movie.com). That may not seem unusual on the surface; but up until he completed this project, Lautman had never been involved in the film industry before.

"People told me I was crazy," Lautman laughs today. "But most of them didn't see what I saw clearly, which was the potential of this project, the movement it could start, and the millions of lives it could impact."

Prior to producing the film, Lautman owned and operated his own sales training company, where he ran in-house training seminars and programs for salespeople. "The business was going well, but I was turning 30, and I [realized] that I could do something much bigger with my life than I had already done," he says.

Strangely, Lautman had always thought that he would be engaged in a film project of some sort. "I didn't know how that was going to show up in my life, but I knew I'd be involved somehow."

Lautman had written many e-books, video training courses, and other materials but had never considered producing a movie. Throughout his career, however, he had seen so many young people breaking the mold in business that it seemed to him that someone needed to tell their stories. "I saw kids making millions of dollars, succeeding and making a difference in creative, unconventional ways," Lautman recalls. "My first thought was to do a book about them." As he thought more deeply about the plan, however, he became convinced that a movie would be more impactful, reaching more of his younger target audience and affecting a much larger group of people.

So he simply got up one day and decided to do it.

He created the plan, found the resources he needed, and made it happen. "Your belief system dictates what you're capable of doing," Lautman says emphatically. The film was shown—among other places—at the legendary Cannes Film Festival in France in 2009. "It's the biggest and best film expo in the world. I believed in this project, and I knew it was that good; so I just said, 'Why not?' and just went ahead and did it."

To further his mission, Lautman founded the Young Entrepreneur Society—an organization that already has thousands of members worldwide—to help people turn their passions into businesses. Y.E.S. makes resources, connections, seminars, and information available to those who want to pursue their dreams of business ownership.

"When I had my small training company, I thought I was big-time, traveling coast-to-coast," recalls Lautman. "Now I'm the founder of an international company, an executive producer of a movie, and a partner with hundreds of people around the globe to inspire others to build their own businesses. All I did was think bigger and act on it—and look what's happening."

DOMINANCE DOESN'T ALWAYS MEAN B-I-G

What is equally as impressive is the fact that within most every organization exists a salesperson or two who does a significant portion of the business within that company. In their own smaller universe, they also qualify as dominant players, unfair-share-getters—800-Pound Gorillas.

Michael J. Malone was a pioneer in what restaurants and retail organizations call "foreground" music, or music used as an integral part of a restaurant or retail store's theme. If you've ever found yourself enjoying the atmosphere of a T.G.I. Friday's, tapped your toes to the beat inside a Starbucks, or gotten lost in the luxury of a Victoria's Secret, you've been captivated by Malone's product; his company, AEI/DMX Music, set the audio stage in these kinds of trendy environments for many years.

Malone started AEI in 1971 using endless-loop, four-hour audio tapes that resembled giant 8-tracks, programmed with the kind of music and tempo that would give the store owners exactly the kind of environment they wanted. AEI became a $100 million company, providing music to major retailers, hotels, restaurants, and the airline industry. The company was sold via merger to Liberty Media in 2001, but in the early days, Malone was the company's number one spokesperson and sales rep.

"There was a point early on where we needed one big client to really give us the momentum we needed to survive," Malone said in a company-wide sales meeting several years ago (at which the author was in attendance). "I had two big meetings that day in the same town, and they were both large casual-dining restaurant clients. If we could get just one of the two to sign up, we'd be okay. If we didn't get either of them, I wasn't sure if we were going to make it."

The two companies' headquarters were across town from one another. Malone went to his morning meeting and gave his best presentation, adding that "Company B across town is doing this, and you need to be on board, too." That wasn't exactly true; Company B's meeting wasn't until that afternoon. "I was so sure they should both be customers that I just got a little ahead of myself," said Malone.

Most of Company A's meeting attendees were fairly uninterested in Malone's presentation—until the mention of the competition, whereupon they sat upright in their chairs and looked around at each other. "We need to do this," they all said, but decided to hold off signing the deal until the end of the day.

Disappointed but undaunted, Malone went across town for his afternoon meeting with Company B, where he mentioned that Company A was lined up with AEI. "They're doing it over there?" they asked. "We can't let them get the jump on us." As Malone left their headquarters with a signed contract, he went to a pay phone to call Company A; they also signed that afternoon.

With the combined weight of both of these trendsetting customers on AEI's client list, business soared. Was Malone nervous that one would call the other? "It was a risk I was willing to take at the time," he said.

Beyond the obvious caveat of stretching the truth, the real lesson to be learned in Mike Malone's example is that 800-Pound Gorillas are always thinking bigger, taking calculated risks, and acting as if they're already there—which allows for success to come that much sooner.

TAKEAWAYS

Thinking Bigger Than Anyone Else

♦ **Being an 800-Pound Gorilla begins by thinking like one.** Those who think small rarely achieve dominant status. When you think bigger, bigger things are naturally attracted to you.

♦ **To become a dominant player, first answer these fundamental questions:**
   ♦ Where do I stand now?

- ◆ Where is my industry going?
- ◆ Do I want to be an 800-Pound Gorilla in that industry?
- ◆ How must I think, and what must I risk, in order to get there?

◆ **Understand and welcome the notion that you can become the dominant player in your specific niche, market, or territory.** You don't have to own the world; you just have to own that corner of the world in which you choose to be the best.

◆ **Don't be afraid to visualize yourself being a bigger player right away.** Think about what being the dominant player in your world would look, feel, smell, taste, and sound like. Gauge how different that is from your current situation today. Measure the gaps that exist between your "today" position and the "dominant tomorrow" position in several categories, and decide what needs to be different in order to achieve a dominant position in each of those categories (quality of service, product performance, product value, and so on).

◆ **Accept and embrace the risks associated with being bigger.** Dominant players are almost always studied, emulated, envied, and criticized. Prepare yourself for that possibility. Ask yourself, "What are the consequences if I *don't* think bigger?" Become comfortable with the feeling of being the dominant player if you're not already.

◆ **If you don't see what needs to exist, create it.** Someone had to be the first in every category, every niche, and every kind of business model. If you discover a market that needs serving, don't be afraid to innovate to serve that need.

2

WHEN YOU'RE REALLY BIG, IT'S HARD TO HIDE ANYWHERE

Why 800-Pound Gorillas Must Be Authentic

What's real?

Coca-Cola has called itself the "Real Thing" for generations. Real numbers are those in mathematics that are both rational and irrational but that actually exist. Real estate refers to land and property that can be valued. Real is also the name of a chain of European superstores, the surname of several soccer teams (such as Real Madrid and Real Salt Lake), and the name of the currency of Brazil.

But what does it *real-ly* mean?

In selling, being real—or *authentic*—is the notion that the way you represent yourself, your company, your product or service is true, factual, and genuine. You're actually who you say you are. You're not putting on a false front, misrepresenting yourself, or purposefully pretending to be something that you're not.

When Andrew Corbus and I sat down to talk about writing our first published book, *Reality Sells* (www.reality sells.com), we wanted to change people's consciousness about the topic of authenticity in business. We convinced many readers that some people in business really don't know who they are, what they stand for, what their best qualities are, or what their customers really like about them. While that may sound crazy, it's important to understand that many business owners—and salespeople—believe that they must be what the customer expects them to be in order to succeed. We found that the exact opposite is true. Those who do know who they are—and aren't afraid to honestly express and use their unique qualities—are the ones who are the most successful and who become the dominant long-term players in their industry.

BETTER TO BE GENUINE

Tim Wackel (www.TimWackel.com) is a very successful sales expert and business speaker from Dallas, Texas, who went from being an electrical engineer who didn't know how to solder to being recognized as the No. 1 sales producer in a 10,000-person sales organization. "Even though I've enjoyed success, some people wouldn't be comfortable saying that they failed at something," admits Wackel. "The bottom line is that it's an authentic part of who I am."

Looking back, Wackel recognizes that he is one of those successful salespeople who rose to prominence primarily by being himself.

"I've not been shy about being genuine and human toward the customers with whom I've worked; and when they find out I'm not perfect, I've found that they're more apt to share things about themselves," says Wackel.

That philosophy was put to the test when Wackel was given a new sales territory that included a problem account—a major telecom customer who was notorious for being very difficult to handle. "He was a hillbilly, buckskin jacket, good-old-boy kind of guy, with a souped-up Mustang and a loud, booming voice," recalls Wackel. "He and I hit it off right from the start. In fact, I couldn't really see what the fuss was all about."

That was, until the day the customer turned on him.

"It was out of the blue," says Wackel. "On our third or fourth meeting, he ripped into me about our product being bad and made demands of our company left and right. It scared me to be in the same office with him." After the client's tirade, Wackel apologized profusely, told him he'd take care of the problems, and quickly left—now understanding what everyone else had been warning him about.

When it came time to revisit his client a few weeks later, it was as if the previous meeting had never happened. "He was just as jovial and happy to see me as the day we met," says Wackel. "Apparently the pattern he had established with the previous reps had been one good meeting to one bad meeting; I was able to get two or three good ones in before he would go ballistic on me."

After several months, the customer's temperamental actions were tearing Wackel up inside. "I couldn't allow it to continue any longer. I'm a straightforward type of guy, and I just decided that I needed to do something."

At their next meeting Wackel sat the client down in his office, closed the door, and said, "I've got to be honest; you're starting to scare me. I come in here and I'm a rock star one day, and the next day you want to shoot me. I don't know if you recognize the differences in our meetings from one to the other, but they're poles apart. It's eating me up—and I want to make it better. Help me understand how we can prevent these cycles from happening. How can we work through this?"

The customer broke down. He told Wackel about his struggles after being diagnosed with multiple personality disorder. He had been wrestling with it for years with a combination of medications and treatments but had not been able to keep it under control. He had also not told a soul about it—up until that moment.

"We were able to work through a lot that day," says Wackel proudly. "He became one of our best customers in the region. After that, we could tell each other anything. He trusted me with that sensitive personal information because I cared enough to bring it up to him. We tossed away those silly customer and sales rep masks, and from then on we were able to talk to each other like human beings and friends."

GERBER GETS IT

Part of Wackel's authenticity is his humility, which he believes is something that's been missing from sales orga-nizations for many years. Another is his passion for energizing others to become successful themselves.

Some others, like my friend Gerber, go even deeper than that.

My family and I met Gerber at Chukka Cove Equestrian Center, located between Ocho Rios and Runaway Bay in Jamaica. We were on a cruise vacation and chose to go horseback riding on the beach as a family while in the port of Ocho Rios. Part of the experience was to ride horseback in water that is chest-deep to the horses, something that was very appealing to my wife, Sherri, an accomplished rider.

Chukka Cove is one of the finest equestrian centers in the Caribbean; and everyone there was very polite, friendly, and accommodating. There were about 25 people in our group that morning including the 5 of us. The facility manager chose the horses that were best suited to the riders' sizes. We each climbed aboard, and the peaceful trail ride part of the trip began.

After 30 minutes or so of trails dotted with dramatic, rocky ocean coves and crashing waves, we stopped at a pavilion where we changed out of our jeans and into our swimsuits and "Jamaican sandals" (bare feet) to prepare for our ride in the ocean. As we rode into the pavilion area, we heard a warm greeting in a thick Jamaican accent:

"Greetings, mon! Are you ready for the ride of your lives?" The young man was beaming and sported large oversized sunglasses, a white T-shirt, and creased shorts. "Welcome to the Chukka Cove pavilion. My name is Gerber, and this is the part you'll remember about Jamaica forever . . . so there's no worries, mon!"

In his charming style, Gerber told us what to expect during this part of the adventure. He explained that we would be riding bareback through the water, and told us

how to control our individual horses through the experience.

"When you get back, you can have a soda or a Red
Stripe beer and talk about your adventure, mon. Gerber is
here to take good care of you."

We had a little bit of a wait, so someone in our group
asked him where the name Gerber had come from.

"It is not my given name. I am 25 years old, and in
Jamaica, typically it is the older men who ask the younger
women for a date. There is a beauuuuutiful woman here on
the island that I asked out, and she was 30 years old. She
said that she would not date someone so young, and so
she called me Gerber, like the Gerber baby on the jars of
baby food." Everyone had a good laugh, including Gerber
himself.

Throughout our brief time at the pavilion, Gerber hap-
pily engaged people one-by-one. He asked their names,
where they were from, and seemed to know a little bit
about every place that was mentioned.

"Have you been to the United States before?" one guest
asked.

"Oh, yes. I've been all around the world. People come
here from everywhere, they take my picture, and take
me home with them; so I'm everywhere!" Everyone was
laughing and enjoying Gerber's enthusiasm for his work.

I asked Gerber how long he had been working at
Chukka Cove. "Two months, mon," he said, and it was
then that I noticed the word "TRAINEE" across the back
of his T-shirt.

"It's not long, but I love my work. I was born and raised
on Jamaica, and I love my homeland. Perhaps you might
consider bringing your family back for a vacation for one,
maybe two weeks soon?"

He wasn't selling me on his equestrian center; he was selling me on his country.

What Gerber understood so well is that Jamaica depends on its customers—tourists—to grow and thrive. He sees his job as something much larger than an employee of the equestrian center; he views his role as being an ambassador for his country. If Jamaican tourism grows, then he and all those around him can grow and prosper together.

What he also brings to his job is his authenticity. Gerber is fun, he's engaging, and he's genuine. The people in our group felt that almost instantly, and truly enjoyed having him around. Although he was "selling" his employer and his country, no one felt like he was selling at all. Gerber brings a refreshing spirit to the concept of selling; and I hope he continues to do it for a long, long time.

While it's important to be authentic, sometimes you have to reassess your current situation and decide if who you are today is who you want to continue to be going forward. What skills should you be focusing on—or not focusing on—to move up and on, while still staying true to yourself?

Michael Soon Lee is a fifth-generation Chinese-American and founder of EthnoConnect—a sales training company that specializes in educating salespeople on how to sell to customers of different cultures. He began his sales career at age 8, when he went door to door selling packets of flower and vegetable seeds from an ad he saw in a comic book. From cookware and magazine subscriptions to remodeling, real estate, and insurance, Michael has encountered success in a number of selling opportunities; and he has always found that one of the keys to his achievements has been his ability to authentically reinvent himself.

"You get into the habit of doing something that works; then after a while, it doesn't work any more," says Lee. "It's important to keep asking, 'What changed?' So many people continue along the same, ineffective path—without bothering to truly assess their situation or without remaining open to change."

Lee was in the southern California real estate business in the mid-1980s when it was announced that the island of Hong Kong would be returned to mainland Chinese ownership in the year 2000. Many Hong Kong residents and businesspeople feared that their asset values would drop steeply because of Communist rule; and so, many investors decided to invest in homes and land in the United States to protect these assets.

Anyone who looked at the situation from the outside saw a virtual gold rush. People from Hong Kong were suddenly interested in buying all kinds of property, especially in the popular Asian market of southern California. Inside, however, there was a problem; many of the deals taking place involved extraordinary negotiations. One Hong Kong buyer would claim that a home was facing the wrong way; but if the owners were to turn their home to the right by, say, 90 degrees, then he might buy today. Several refused to buy unless the owners took steps to remove the number 4 from their address. Real estate professionals were frustrated, because they were simply not versed in Chinese cultural norms like *feng shui* or the significance of certain numbers representing good or bad luck.

Several Chinese customers initially saw Michael, who looked to be a fellow countryman, as someone who could help them. The problem was that Michael was fully steeped in U.S. culture. He couldn't speak any of the Chinese languages; in fact, the only thing he knew how to say in Chinese was "I don't speak Chinese."

"The Chinese had a word for people like me," he says. "It's pronounced jook-sing. The literal translation means empty head, but the Chinese understand it to mean a person who has lost his culture over a period of time." And it was true. He was just as American—and, in the Chinese buyers' minds, uneducated—as all the other agents.

"It was at that point that I decided that I needed to learn more about my own culture," says Michael. So he read books and went to local classes on Chinese culture. He quickly learned what he was doing wrong, and what he needed to do to serve these customers with respect for how they see the world. He reached out to the Chinese buyers once again, and this time, was very successful in helping them buy properties.

Several real estate agents saw what Michael was doing and asked if he would teach them what he had learned. He put together a small class for the other agents, and began teaching it on the side. Word soon spread of Michael's unique class for the real estate industry—and it began to grow.

Agents then began to ask Michael if he could teach a class on the Hispanic culture. Michael explains, "It seemed kind of crazy at the time, but once again, I found myself needing to be willing to change and look at the opportunities. I did the research on the Hispanic culture, combined it with the basic knowledge I had about the subject, and created a similar class for selling real estate to Hispanic customers." It was a similar program that asked the same basic questions: How do Hispanics buy homes differently—and how can we as real estate agents understand that culture and respond in a way that's respectful of it?

By using the techniques that he was teaching others, Michael soon became a million-dollar producer in real estate, and grew to own a real estate brokerage firm with more than 50 agents. Eventually, Michael sold the firm to concentrate solely on educating others in the ways of other cultures. Today, Michael is *the* subject matter expert on selling to multicultural customers; he has written six books on the subject, his company is in high demand, and he has a busy worldwide schedule of speaking and training. His business has expanded to the sales component of nearly every industry—including new car sales, insurance, food service, retail, and financial services.

GETTING INTO THE LEARNING HABIT

Michael has found that those who are constantly studying and learning are automatically more authentic with others. "Just [as it is] in dealing with people of other cultures—the more you know, the less you have to pretend you know," he says. "In any kind of sales, reading from a script is like pretending you care. If the words aren't yours, they won't come [across] as truly genuine, and prospects pick up on that very quickly."

In addition to being a successful real estate broker and entrepreneur, Michael Soon Lee is a former stage and screen actor. He has appeared in movies such as *Foul Play*, starring Chevy Chase and Goldie Hawn, and *Die Laughing*, with former teen star Robby Benson. He has had to read through his share of 300-page scripts, and he says that the best actors don't always memorize every line verbatim.

"When I would study for a scene, I would ask myself, 'What is this scene trying to convey? What is the *intent* of the words that were written for me to say?' I would then do my best to deliver what the director of the scene was intending for the scene to convey. Quite often, the director doesn't care what words you use. What they really want is for you to deliver the *intent;* and sometimes that means using your own words."

A GENUINE CONTRARIAN

Being authentic doesn't mean you can't be creative in your approach. On the contrary, if you're a creative type, being noncreative would be—well, unauthentic.

Sean McPheat is founder and managing director of international sales training firm MTD Sales Training (www.mtdsalestraining.com). McPheat is widely regarded as the United Kingdom's No. 1 authority on modern day selling, having been featured in more than 200 different publications and TV appearances as an expert in the field of personal and professional development.

McPheat says that the United Kingdom's sales training style is still rather stuffy. "Most everyone who does what I do is wearing a formal, dark-colored suit and conservative tie," he says. "I was doing that, too, and at some point, I asked myself, 'Why am I doing training this way, when I'm actually more creative and free-spirited than this?'"

He took a page from the playbooks of local business icons Gordon Ramsey and Richard Branson, and decided to become more authentic—by having fun with his authentic persona. "I wanted to be known as a fun-loving brand. I'm very serious about sales success, but I don't take myself too seriously, and so I re-created my own personal brand in a fun, bold sort of way."

McPheat, who is distinctively bald and wears a slight goatee, hired a publicist and an artist to help him rebrand himself. He had caricatures drawn of himself as a Jedi knight made famous in the movies of *Star Wars*, with a light saber slicing through sales objections like "not now," "no money," and "the economy," and branded himself as Master of the Sales Force.

He had a caricature drawn of him as a boxer, hoisting a large title belt next to a ring announcer, holding his hand upward in victory and proclaiming him "the undisputed heavyweight champion of the world" when it comes to selling to the buyer of today.

"When I do keynote speeches now, I come onstage with a light saber and a *Star Wars* kind of theme," McPheat laughs. "It's very different, but it's very memorable, especially here in the U.K., where most others just don't choose to go in a creative direction."

McPheat admits that the new Sean has met with mixed reactions. "They either love it or hate it, but that's okay. I would rather have that kind of response than be boring and have no response at all. The bottom line is that it's memorable; those that like it truly like it, and it's been fantastic for my business." Potential clients and media contacts now call him far more often than before, and specifically ask for "the Sales Jedi guy."

"Sometimes in a competitive situation you don't need to be better," McPheat offers. "You just need to be different."

In a genuine sort of way.

TAKEAWAYS

Being Authentic

◆ **True 800-Pound Gorillas are real, genuine, and authentic to everyone around them.** Dominant companies and individuals don't have to be someone they're not in order to achieve their success. They know themselves well. They're comfortable with their image, and portray themselves in an accurate way; their message is not overblown, unclear, or incorrect.

♦ **Prospects can tell when you're being authentic.** Consumers are wiser today than they've ever been, and their BS meters are on at all times. Sales pros are at their best when their core values, skills, and knowledge align to help a prospect realize the benefits of their product or service. That only happens when a salesperson is demonstrating his or her genuine self in the interaction.

♦ **Authenticity works best in sales if it illuminates a clear difference between you and the competition.** Many industries have certain standards of decorum and behavior, which may inhibit some people from fully using and exploiting their genuine personality; however, if you can find a way to be yourself, celebrate it, and make it your point of differentiation. It can be a very powerful tool in becoming a more dominant player.

♦ **Your authentic self of today may change and evolve over time.** All of us are changing, evolving, and growing, and depending on your circumstances, your desire to be one thing may change to become another. That's okay; the best are always looking to grow, and the best you can do is to be true to yourself in deciding which direction to take at any given time.

♦ **Listen to your conscience when determining your authentic self.** Dominance doesn't have to mean illicitly profiting at the expense of others. The decision to do right by others allows you the freedom to develop into your authentic self, without the guilt or other shackles that may get in the way of your eventual success. There are plenty of dominant players who got there by being crooked, ruthless, and cold-hearted; you don't have to be one of them.

THANK YOU,
AMERICAN TOURISTER

Why 800-Pound Gorillas Get to
Rattle the Cage

In the 1970s and '80s, American Tourister Luggage ran a memorable commercial demonstrating the durability of its product. The spot showed a zookeeper tossing a red American Tourister suitcase into a crazed gorilla's cage while the gorilla did everything in his power to try to destroy the piece of luggage—throwing it, tossing it, jumping up and down on it, banging it noisily into the bars of his cage, and roaring angrily all the while.

(Do gorillas not like luggage? Are they disturbed by the color red? Did he actually scream like a banshee throughout the filming, or was the sound dubbed in? By the way, once again, the stereotype of the gorilla is badly exaggerated, adding fuel to the fire that gorillas are aggressive by nature . . . but I digress.)

The announcer's voiceover during this 30-second suitcase assault was read like a letter to various groups of people, and it went like this: "Dear clumsy bellboys . . . brutal cab drivers . . . careless doormen . . . ruthless porters . . . savage baggage masters . . . and bald, butterfingered luggage handlers all over the world. Have we got a suitcase for you!" The American Tourister name was then superimposed on the screen and the gorilla shown leaving the outside viewing area of his cage, dragging the intact, unscathed suitcase behind him.

The story behind the ad—which most people never knew—was that the "gorilla" was not a gorilla at all. Inside the hairy gorilla suit was actually actor Don McLeod, whose elaborate costume had moveable eyelids, mouth, brow, and lips, which allowed him to mimic emotions with his face.

The ad ran for 15 years, and lifted American Tourister to a position of dominance in the luggage category in the United States. The gorilla campaign was named one of the Top 100 advertisements of the twentieth century by *Advertising Age* magazine, and is still remembered today by many.

The ad did two things for American Tourister: It left an indelible impression in the minds of those consumers who wanted a durable suitcase that would withstand the assault it would receive at the airport; and it also gave the company the perception of brand dominance—just like the gorilla gives the impression of dominance—in the world of luggage. The gorilla and the suitcase became linked; you could not think of one without the other.

It's the ad that gave American Tourister its 800-Pound Gorilla status.

By showing its product's durability in a graphic, memorable way, American Tourister was, literally, rattling the cage. The company shook up the market; by airing that ad, it was daring anyone else to put its suitcase in that cage and see how long it lasted.

SHAKE IT UP, BABY

Dominant players aren't afraid to put their products to the test. Because of their size, they also have the ability to shake things up. When the U.S. Congress introduced legislation in 2009 to make it easier for unions to organize in their workplaces, Federal Express took action. As an 800-Pound Gorilla in the package delivery industry, FedEx was primarily a nonunion company; of its 290,000 workers, only its 4,700 pilots were unionized. The company's chief rival in the United States was United Parcel Service, which had about 55 percent of its 425,000 employees as members of a labor union, mainly Teamsters. While unions are one way of guaranteeing employees fair wages and safe working conditions, unionization generally means higher costs of doing business overall; and FedEx did not want any further unionization of its employees if it could help it.

So the company rattled the cage.

FedEx is a big customer of the airplane industry. Boeing, a U.S. manufacturer of airplanes, was one of FedEx's main suppliers of new planes for its fleet in 2009; and FedEx had a tentative order for 30 brand-new B777F planes from Boeing. The company exercised an option to buy 15 of them with another option to buy 15 more. On March 25, 2009, FedEx announced that it would consider canceling its order with Boeing—a contract worth anywhere from $5 billion to $7 billion—if Congress were to pass the union bill. A FedEx spokesman was quoted as saying the legislation had the potential to lethally damage the company financially, which would make it "exceedingly unlikely that we would purchase those airplanes."

The Teamsters union, staunch backers of the bill, shouted back. Its spokesmen accused FedEx of blackmailing Congress and further weakening the economy with its threat. The Teamsters had been trying to unionize FedEx's employees for years, and saw the bill as a golden opportunity to finally bring FedEx into the fold. The Teamsters saw FedEx's announcement as putting unfair pressure on Congress to stop the union bill from passing.

You can only play a card like that if you're an 800-Pound Gorilla.

KNOW WHEN TO HOLD 'EM ...

For those who want to become a dominant player like a Federal Express, however, it's a good idea to demonstrate your muscle carefully.

"We rarely do that sort of thing," explains Barry Huebner. Huebner is president of Midwest Transit Equipment, a major dealer of new and preowned commercial buses. As one of the 800-Pound Gorillas of school buses, shuttle buses, charter buses, and minibuses, it commands between 50 and 90 percent of the market in areas of Illinois and Indiana, and does business in nearly all 50 states and internationally. "In my opinion, you can't play that card more than once; otherwise, you become labeled as someone who's difficult to work with," Huebner says.

Huebner said Midwest Transit is thought of differently. "We may be a major player in our business, but our customers and suppliers consider us more as partners. You can't do that by rattling the saber all the time."

Where Midwest Transit's status really helps, however, is in allowing it to come through for its clients in ways that others may not. "Because of our volume, sometimes we can work with our manufacturers to get a more favorable delivery slot for a key customer. We may also agree with a manufacturer to buy buses that will be built in their off-seasons, which keeps their workers on the assembly line and allows us to pass along some unique cost savings."

Another advantage Midwest Transit can realize for its customers includes rush delivery of spare parts. "If we ask for something special, they may be able to prioritize it for us because of the volume we represent to them," Huebner shares. "If it allows us to help our customers, we want to try to make it happen—and our suppliers understand this, too, so they're willing to help." The company doesn't abuse its favored status, so when it does ask, it's usually because it really needs to.

Because his company is careful to develop good partnerships, Huebner is particularly sensitive to others who attempt to rattle the cage with them. "We've had a few situations where some of our partners have made competitive decisions that haven't been in our best mutual interest," Huebner admits. "As much as we don't want to, sometimes you have to get up and take a stand."

IT TAKES CONFIDENCE

Midwest Transit chooses to develop relationships rather than flex its muscles. If you're the kind of entity that *has* muscle, however, and are confident about the message you want to deliver, there are ways in which 800-Pound Gorillas have been known to do that, too.

In the fall of 1985, the Chicago Bears were emerging as the team to beat in the National Football League (NFL). Its cast of characters included the mohawk-wearing quarterback Jim McMahon, 330-pound William "The Refrigerator" Perry, Hall of Fame running back Walter Payton, intense middle linebacker Mike Singletary, and "The Coach," Chicago legend Mike Ditka.

The Bears came from behind to win their season opener against Tampa Bay, 38–28, which started a 12-game winning streak that included shutouts against Dallas and Atlanta and dominant performances against nearly every other team. Their first loss of the season, against the Miami Dolphins in the Orange Bowl on December 2, would be their only loss of the season, en route to a 46–10 Super Bowl shellacking of the New England Patriots in Super Bowl XX.

Ironically, it was the day after their loss to the Dolphins that several Bears players got together to record a song that would go down in history as one of the boldest cage-rattling public predictions ever made by a professional sports team. Randy Weigand, a record producer, friend of wide receiver Willie Gault, and boyfriend of one of the Chicago Bears cheerleaders, had an idea to create a song and a music video to market the Bears and their success on the field. Proceeds from the recording would go to a local food pantry, which appealed to many of the players who participated, especially the philanthropic-minded Payton.

"The Super Bowl Shuffle" was recorded in a single day, featuring 10 Bears players rapping fun, bold lyrics about their abilities on the field and their confidence in bringing home a Super Bowl championship. Their rap was backed up by additional Bears players, the "Shufflin' Crew" playing various instruments and dancing along on the music video.

The song was rushed to local radio stations, and was an immediate hit in Midwest markets. It quickly climbed to as high as number 41 on Billboard's Top 100 Songs in the nation, and with a few games still left in the regular season, the Bears now had to back up their words with actions.

The chorus to the "Super Bowl Shuffle" didn't exactly guarantee a championship, but some of the players' lyrics made it seem like a foregone conclusion. Payton, known as "Sweetness", rapped about their goal of giving Chicago "a Super Bowl champ." Richard Dent suggested that Chicagoans "had better start makin' their Super Bowl plans." Each player on the recording had similar lyrics, all in fun, and all with the same theme: We're a team of destiny, and we're going all the way.

A few well-known Bears players, including Hall of Fame defensive end Dan Hampton, chose not to participate, thinking it was too overconfident.

Was it too bold? Should someone from the Bears organization have stepped in? What sort of fallout would there have been if the Bears didn't wind up winning it all? Did the fact that the prediction was made on vinyl motivate them to make it happen that much more? Those are the kinds of risks that cage-rattlers must be willing to accept to rise up to—or solidify—their dominant status.

Other NFL teams have tried to mirror the Bears' idea with little success. In 1986, both the Los Angeles Raiders and the Los Angeles Rams took a stab at their own music video prediction songs, but neither team won so much as a single playoff game. In 1999, the Jacksonville Jaguars recorded, "Uh Oh, The Jaguars Super Bowl Song," only to lose in the American Football Conference Championship game.

The "Super Bowl Shuffle" stands alone as the only musical sports prediction that rattled the cage and actually lived up to its expectations.

OFFENSE, DEFENSE, AND COMMON SENSE

The Chicago Bears stuck their necks out in a big way by predicting a Super Bowl victory. Conventional wisdom would tell you that it isn't wise to fire up the opposing teams that way, but the Bears felt that they could back it up with action.

Whether on the playing field or the field of life, going against conventional wisdom can appear to others as cage-rattling—and in order to get their point across, some 800-Pound Gorillas have used a well-placed dose of common sense.

Dave Ramsey is a financial author, radio and television host, and motivational speaker. His three-hour syndicated radio program, *The Dave Ramsey Show*, is heard Monday through Friday by nearly 4 million listeners on over 400 radio stations across North America. In the words of Ramsey's web site (www.daveramsey.com), the show "focuses on life, love and relationships, and how they happen to revolve around money." His program is also on Sirius/XM Satellite Radio, as well as appearing as a regular televised segment on Fox Business Network. His best-selling books include *Financial Peace* and *More than Enough*.

Ramsey's commonsense views of less conspicuous consumption, more saving, and getting out of debt are widely praised by those who understand how money works, but are not widely adopted in most people's lifestyles. Ramsey's life work is, in his words, "to teach others how to be financially responsible, so they can acquire enough wealth to take care of loved ones, live prosperously into old age, and give generously to others."

In order to get his point across, Ramsey often has to rattle the cage with his callers.

A large part of Ramsey's program is taking phone calls from all over the country, with listeners' questions on everything from what to do with a $2,000 car loan in a divorce case to paying off half-million-dollar mortgages. "Debt is dumb, cash is king and the paid-off mortgage has taken the place of the BMW as the status symbol of choice," Ramsey proclaims at the opening of each of his radio programs. "If you're winning, we're gonna win with you. If you're struggling, we want to help you win."

By taking calls from real listeners with real problems, and helping them solve those problems by asking them what are often difficult and revealing personal questions, Ramsey is getting his message across to not only the individual caller, but the thousands of other listeners who may be going through similar dilemmas in their lives. "Sometimes we have to take you by the shoulders and shake you up—ask you some tough questions on this program," Ramsey says to his audience during a recent radio show. "We assume that when you call, you're gonna be okay with that. It may even be why you called in the first place!"

As a dominant voice in the media, Dave Ramsey is doing right by his callers, one at a time—and doing right by his many listeners at the same time—by rattling the cage to get his callers and his audience to see the light.

TAKEAWAYS

Rattling the Cage

♦ **The 800-Pound Gorillas of the world are the ones who can rattle the cage and attract significant attention to their cause, if necessary.** When you wield enough influence in the marketplace to affect a major change, alter policy, or challenge steadfast traditions, rattling the cage may prove to be a beneficial thing to do.

♦ **Cage-rattlers get their message across in a bold way.** Whether it's a cause, a point of view, a proposal, or a solution, 800-Pound Gorillas aren't afraid to be heard.

♦ **Cage-rattlers need not be mean-spirited.** The information or help that you supply by rattling the cage can actually be in the best interest of those who you're targeting. By virtue of your dominant position, however, it may be construed as domineering, heavy-handed, or forced. Be aware of this, and use caution in how you choose to act.

♦ **Dominant players should rattle the cage only when necessary.** Excessive use of cage-rattling techniques are ill-advised, because they tend to color you or your business in an unfavorable light long-term. When there is mutual interest in standing up for something, however, such as using your dominant status as a way of going to bat for a customer on occasion, it's one of the highest and best uses of your status.

4

NO ONE'S EVER DONE IT BEFORE

Why 800-Pound Gorillas Do What Others Won't

Saint Joseph's College is a Division II Catholic liberal arts institution in Rensselaer, Indiana (www.saintjoe.edu). It's a school with a proud heritage of small average class sizes (14), unique curriculums, and the opportunity to excel in a small campus environment. Founded in 1889 by the Missionaries of the Precious Blood (C.PP.S.), the school's 180 acres are host to around 1,000 students each year. Its beautiful, park-like campus was the home of the Chicago Bears training camp from 1944 through 1974, and was featured in the classic movie, *Brian's Song*.

When I moved into Bennett Hall as a freshman at SJC in 1979, there wasn't much going on in the small town of

Rensselaer. For after-class fun off campus, students could choose from the bowling alley, the Wagon Wheel Bar & Grill, Pizza Hut, and the Tastee-Freez. The town didn't have a T-shirt store, a sporting goods retailer, or a McDonald's within the city limits.

Which suited me just fine.

I really didn't want to get a job on campus, but I needed a way to earn some money. In that first month in school, I quickly learned that intramural athletics were very popular. More than 20 different sports were offered, spread out over two different semesters, and everyone participated. I also learned that if all those intramural teams wanted to get T-shirts or jerseys printed for their teams, they had to go out of town—because there was no sporting goods store or T-shirt place in town. Even the campus bookstore, a small retailer that carried some printed school merchandise, didn't offer lettering or numbering.

Why hasn't anyone seen the need and done something about it? I thought to myself. And so, as a student entrepreneur, I saw an opportunity.

I had considered opening up a T-shirt shop of my own at a young age and actually owned a commercial heat-transfer iron—the kind you might see at a sports store or T-shirt shop that would apply those large decals from the '70s, or put vinyl letters onto the backs of T-shirts or jerseys. I decided that there was enough demand to go into business for myself. And so the W/B Custom Shirtworks was born in October 1979 in a dorm room with a single iron and a few boxes of 2-inch vinyl letters.

"You can't open up a business while you're in school," my college friends said. "You'll be too busy with school work. You need capital and inventory. You need advertising. There's no way."

I decided that they were wrong. I knew the demand was there; I just needed to fill it.

Once word got out about my new venture, the orders came in quickly; soon I was cranking out dozens of jerseys and T-shirts every month. I did custom designs for teams that students couldn't even get from their hometown T-shirt shops and turned them around quickly. Because the different intramural sports overlapped, there was always a league starting at any given time. During busy times, I was up until all hours of the night, pressing T-shirts and sending up a puff of smoke after every shirt had "cooked" long enough. (I can't believe my roommate, Ted Sinal, put up with me for four years of that awful smell of burning vinyl.) After my freshman year, with a year of successful entrepreneurship under my belt, I tackled a potentially large account with an idea.

Up until 1979, the intramural champions from each sport had always received small, cheap plastic trophies for winning. I thought we needed to change that, so I did what no one else had done: I asked the person in charge to consider changing the award policy.

I made an appointment with the school's director of recreation to pitch my idea. "Your plastic trophies are okay," I said, "but they just sit on someone's dresser. An Intramural Champion T-shirt, however, would be something the winners could wear proudly all around campus." I showed him a T-shirt design template I had created for my presentation. "I can design and print T-shirts that look like this—'SJC Intramural Champion—1980-1981', and insert the appropriate sport figure—whether it's a tennis player, basketball player, or whatever—in the design, so that the shirts are unique to each sport. I'll keep a supply of these shirts on hand in my inventory, so we can custom-print each sport's champions' shirts based on their sizes and have them in their hands no more than 24 hours after they win—all for about the same price you're paying for trophies now."

I got the contract, and I printed several hundred shirts each year, which were much more enthusiastically received and worn all over campus with pride.

By the end of my college career, I had designed, printed, and sold thousands of garments; and on my last day of school, turned down an offer from the head of the SJC School of Business to buy my company.

I should have sold it while I had the chance.

THE "DOING" SETS YOU APART

Someone who decides to become an 800-Pound Gorilla often succeeds because he or she has chosen to do what others won't. They go the extra mile, do a little bit more, and humble themselves to take on whatever additional role they need to take to satisfy those they serve. Others may think it's crazy, but a true dominant player knows that it's often the little points of differentiation that make a big difference—such as:

♦ Visiting a construction site and preparing an extra set of blueprints for a bid.
♦ Researching several options for a prospect, and delivering the results.
♦ Driving to several of the prospect's locations to train the employees on a product's proper use at no additional cost.
♦ Delivering additional value to an agreement beyond the scope of the project.

- ◆ Creating a sample product, customized for the prospect.
- ◆ Sending a thank-you gift to those who helped you secure the business.
- ◆ Referring a prospect to another vendor that better fits their needs and scope for a certain project.
- ◆ Supplying a little something extra that delights a prospect.

When I worked at radio station WKAN, we ran some of the best golf outings in the county. This was thanks to the genius of our station manager—and avid golfer—Gary Wright, who believed that a golf outing needed to be memorable, fun, and different. Our best advertisers were invited to play, and we prepared several value-added things for them throughout the day: game show-type events at the turn, unique contests, great prizes, and one-of-a-kind participation events.

Of all the things we did, Gary was perhaps most proud of an idea he had seen down South that he brought to our annual event: a mid-round opportunity to refresh a golfer's face with a small, washcloth-sized towel that had been drenched in ice water, so cold that small icicles were clinging to the towel material. A small amount of mango scent was placed in the water, so when a golfer was presented with the opportunity for a "nice mango towel," the experience was heavenly. The WKAN representative used tongs to dip into a special cooler that was stacked with these super cool washcloths, and on a hot day on the course, those "nice mango towels" were one of the most delightfully unexpected extras that we heard about most often from our participants.

So what could *you* do to become a more dominant salesperson that others won't, can't, or don't choose to do?

GIVE AWAY VALUABLE INFORMATION

The Internet has become the research tool of choice worldwide, and many 800-Pound Gorillas have used this aspect of the Web to build their business to dominance. Some companies cringe at the thought of putting their valuable information on the Web for all to see; while others see it as a decidedly Gorilla-like move. For example, Longfellow Benefits—an employee benefits broker and consultant in Boston—has a web site chock full of advice, information, and key data regarding insurance and benefits for small to medium-sized businesses (www.LongfellowBenefits.com).

"Some would say that we're giving our product away for free," says Craig Cerretani, one of Longfellow's principals and founders. "If our only product was information, they'd be right. Our basic premise is this: People are smart. We provide them with stuff they can use for free; and as a result, we become the expert for them. We educate people. We [believe] in our deliverables and our ability to execute—so much so that we know that after we've educated someone, we'll be in the running for the business when the time comes."

How about giving away *more* information for free? Longfellow also offers free webinars—often in conjunction with other complementary professional firms in the area—on key subjects of interest in the employee benefits world. Craig explains, "Recently, we partnered with a local law firm to do a webinar on some changes that we knew were coming from the government regarding the Family Medical Leave Act. FMLA is a major concern to most every employer, and we knew these changes were significant, so we quickly put together a joint presentation to let participants know what was coming."

Longfellow marketed the webinar via e-mail to its current client database and key prospects—as well as the law firm's database and prospects—which effectively doubled its reach—and its potential to attract new clients.

"The webinar attracted 120 participants, many of whom sent in questions during the program," says Cerretani. "Those numbers were very good for us, and it was obviously an important topic in the minds of those who called in." The program was free, but participants were required to type in their contact information prior to their participation. That information became solid gold for both Longfellow and the law firm. According to Cerretani, "We followed up on every single one and just started a conversation. We asked things like, 'Did you get anything from the webinar?', 'Is your current benefits provider doing things like this for you?', and 'What would it feel like to do business with Longfellow?' It was all just a conversation, and many of those conversations have turned into major business deals for us." Longfellow now does five or six webinars a year, all on different topics relative to today's most critical issues regarding employee benefits.

Cerretani may be on to something; business at Longfellow was up 40 percent in 2008.

CREATE OPPORTUNITIES FOR OTHERS

Bryant Pfeiffer is considered one of the best in the professional sports business at season and group ticket sales.

For five years he was a record-breaking season ticket and group sales rep for the Minnesota Timberwolves of the National Basketball Association (NBA). He personally sold over 3,000 season tickets in the first-year launch of the Minnesota Lynx—the Timberwolves' sister team in the Women's National Basketball Association (WNBA). As sales manager for both these teams, Pfeiffer and his reps consistently outperformed others, and the Lynx led the entire WNBA in group ticket sales in 2007.

"I always have my antennas up," says Pfeiffer, now a national senior director of team services for Major League Soccer. "I encourage all the reps that I work with today in MLS to look for ideas everywhere. There are creative opportunities right in front of you; you just have to train yourself to think creatively and look for them."

Case in point: In 2007, Ricky Davis was a Timberwolves player with an overly confident, slightly colorful self-image. "Ricky would just say things that he should have thought through a little better," says Pfeiffer, "and he really struck a nerve after the Portland game."

It was early in the 2007 NBA basketball season. The T-Wolves were playing on the road against the Portland Trail Blazers, a young, scrappy team, and it was an intense game that went into overtime. Afterward, Davis was answering questions from the media about the play of the Blazers.

"Those guys are a bunch of cockroaches," he said. "They were everywhere!"

The media, of course, was all over Davis's comment, stirring the ire of the Portland team and creating a mini-rivalry that would spill over into the Blazers' next game with Minnesota—which just happened to be two weeks later in Minneapolis.

"People were angry in Portland," recalls Pfeiffer. "It was not a flattering comment at all, and the media was fanning the flames. I thought it was an opportunity for someone to have a little fun at the upcoming game in Minneapolis." But with only two weeks to go, Pfeiffer had to act quickly. "I thought of all the tie-ins for cockroaches and came up with an idea for a group outing for a local pest control company. The idea was to have all the employees of the pest control company come out to a game wearing their extermination gear from their jobs to be there to wipe out the 'cockroaches' from Portland. It would be a memorable night out for the company's employees; and there was a strong chance that the local media would pick up on the story for additional exposure."

Pfeiffer quickly got on the phone and arranged a 10-minute face-to-face meeting with the president of a large local pest control company in the Twin Cities area. "She was not a sports fan, which made it more challenging," says Pfeiffer, "but I didn't let that get in the way." He presented the press clippings about the cockroach comment, the stir it had caused, and the idea he had. "This president had never even touched a basketball before, much less been a fan," recalls Pfeiffer, "but I painted a picture of what a unique opportunity this was for her. I said, 'This cockroach theme is a once-in-a-generation opportunity. Imagine 500 to 1,000 of your employees in their uniforms, with their hats on, in the Target Center arena with all the TV cameras and local media there covering the game, talking about the cockroach incident, and seeing all your people there. Not only will it improve the morale and team spirit of your employees; the incremental exposure you'll receive in the press is a huge PR opportunity for you.'"

Thanks to Pfeiffer's enthusiasm, the president agreed. Five hundred exterminators in full uniform attended the game that night, and the media did cover the funny follow-up to the cockroach story, noting the pest control company by name.

"It's important to remember that their people had a great time as well," adds Pfeiffer. "It wasn't just a publicity stunt. The employees were grateful to the company for the opportunity to be treated to a game. It was a win-win-win all around."

To find similar ideas and opportunities, Pfeiffer reads the newspaper and scours the media for new potential material every day. "It's amazing what you'll find if you just open your eyes and ears to the possibilities."

For example, a local Twin Cities resident had been interviewed on local media as a multiday contestant on the *Jeopardy!* game show on which he had won a considerable amount of money. The newspaper asked him what he planned to do with his winnings, and, being a local sports fan, he mentioned that he wanted to buy season tickets to the Minnesota Wild, the local National Hockey League (NHL) team.

"The minute I read that, I got fired up," Pfeiffer says. "I had to track this guy down. If he had the means to buy Wild season tickets, I was going to sell him on Timberwolves season tickets as well." Pfeiffer found the man's contact information and called him at home. "I left a message on his voice mail telling him that I was Bryant from the Minnesota Timberwolves, and I had some exciting news for him," Pfeiffer recalls. "He called back, thinking I was just another publicity interview, but I told him that I had seen him on TV and in the newspaper, and since he was a local celebrity, I wanted to treat him and a friend to a VIP night at a T-Wolves game as my guest." Being a basketball fan as well, the man gladly accepted.

The game gave Pfeiffer a great opportunity to sit down with the *Jeopardy!* contestant and get to know him. He asked several questions about what it was like backstage on the game show. "Eventually, I wanted to see if he'd consider becoming a T-Wolves season ticket holder," says Pfeiffer. "I didn't mention that I had heard the comment about the hockey tickets, and asked him what sorts of plans he had for the money. He told me about the Wild but ended up buying season tickets from me as well."

Like all 800-Pound Gorillas, Pfeiffer looks for ways to sell whenever and wherever he can, even in the most unusual places and circumstances. While one particular instance that Pfeiffer recalls may have crossed the line—looking back, he says he'd do it all over again.

Pfeiffer and his wife were invited to the wedding of one of his wife's friends from high school. As the ceremony went on, Pfeiffer recognized the name of the father of the bride as one of the people he had been chasing to buy Timberwolves season tickets but had not been able to reach to close the deal. "He had gone dark, which is a term we use for people who were hot to buy at one point and just disappear or become impossible to reach. I had talked to him several times, and we knew each other from the phone conversations we had had but had never met face-to-face."

Pfeiffer got the chance he was looking for during the receiving line at the reception. "I went up to him and introduced myself. He instantly recognized my name, so in a fun way, I leaned in to him and asked, 'So how many seats do you want?' He probably thought I was a wedding crasher at first; but after he learned that I was legit, he gave me his credit card number that night!"

Pfeiffer believes you've got to be crazy enough to ask the question. "What do I have to lose? What's the worst that can happen?" he asks. "Everywhere I'd go, I'd constantly be asking, 'Who can I talk to about seats?' It became a game, an obsession, but in a fun way."

Sports ticket sales reps are at their busiest during game nights, greeting the customers they've sold, cultivating new relationships, seating VIPs or working with groups to make sure all the details are taken care of. One of the jobs often not worked most effectively is the table at the stadium where a team will sell its season ticket packages to the new customers who are in the arena.

"It's the biggest potential pool of prospects that you'll ever find," says Pfeiffer emphatically. "They're all right there; they're interested in the team enough to come to a game, so they're the very best leads for a ticket package. And yet, some reps will sit behind the table, sit on their hands, and not reach out to people as they walk past. They look bored, and they're probably scaring people away."

Pfeiffer made it a point to work as many of those opportunities as possible. "I took the sales shifts at the table as often as I could. When the team went on outreach programs to promote the brand, I signed up to go to every fair, every expo, every outside event we had on the schedule. I worked hard to meet everyone, asking questions, finding out more, and getting business cards. Lots of those contacts were eventually turned into sales."

Pfeiffer now trains others to do what he did so successfully, and he encourages them to create fun games and contests while working a booth or table. "Don't ever stand behind the table," Pfeiffer advises. "Always stand in front, so that you can engage people where they are instead of approaching them from behind something. If you have something in quantity—like a printed brochure or a game schedule— hand them out to people as they pass by."

Pfeiffer and his staff even created a slew of contests to keep everyone at the booth engaged. "We did challenges with each other, like 'How Long Can You Hold a Conversation?', where you actually time how long someone spends with a prospect, and the loser buys lunch. We had a business card collection contest. We played the 'Look-Alike Game,' where we look at people and try to think of who they look like—anything to keep us all engaged and having fun. No one wants to come up to the Dull Table and say hello."

Being outgoing didn't come naturally for Pfeiffer. "I'm very intense, but inside, I'm actually a fairly low-key guy. For me to succeed, I knew I had to become more outgoing, so I took a class in improvisational comedy. I learned a ton about how to get out of my shell, how to engage people, have fun with them, and how to hold their attention."

Even when he wasn't working a table, Pfeiffer was in a suit and tie for game nights, and, with his team lanyard around his neck, he was constantly fielding questions from fans about where things are. "They saw I had the suit on, so they assumed that I was somebody who knew something," Pfeiffer laughs. "But if someone is asking me a question, it's a great opportunity for me to get the fan talking about their experience with the team, who they like on the team, what they do for a living, and eventually lead to a question about season tickets."

His standard response to a question is almost always the same. "If someone is looking for directions, my first response is, 'Oh, is this your first time in the arena?' If it is, it inevitably leads to questions about how they got their tickets, if they're big fans, and if they've ever considered the options and the benefits of being a season ticket holder.

"It's that little bit extra," Pfeiffer admits. "It's amazing to me how much more success people could bring to themselves if they would just decide to do that little extra ask."

ALWAYS BEING AROUND

Most salespeople give up after the first or second call. But 800-Pound Gorillas understand that the first or second call is just the beginning.

Recent statistics from Dartnell Corporation, a leading publisher of business information and training resources (www.dartnell.com), reveal that of those who decide to quit calling on a particular prospect—48 percent do so after the first sales call, 24 percent after the second, 12 percent after the third, 6 percent after the fourth, and 10 percent after the fifth call or later. This means that most sales reps—over 70 percent—stop calling after only *two* attempts. In other words, you can differentiate yourself immediately by simply making sure that you call someone at least three times before you give up on them.

In a portion of my work as a speaker and seminar leader, I sell my own services by calling executive-level sales directors of professional sports teams. This group of people is among the busiest and most difficult to reach, and even though I leave several voice mails with my prospects, these executives rarely return my calls. It isn't because I'm not a valuable contact for them; it's just that the urgency of the day is more of a priority to them than my product. Because of that, I always try to call these people back every two or three days after leaving my first voice mail. It may persist for a few weeks, a few months, or sometimes longer.

My persistence has become one of my dominant success qualities. It may seem excessive to some, but I've lost track of the number of executives who have told me, "Hey, Bill, thanks for your persistence. I really appreciate it."

No one says, "Man, I wish that guy would leave me alone," or at least no one has said that to me in person. That's because they understand that I'm doing my job—which is selling my services to them with the understanding that although I'm not their top priority, I'm a priority nonetheless—and I'll do what it takes to reach them.

TAKE MORE RISKS THAN OTHERS

All 800-Pound Gorillas are driven—because they know great things are done by those who are willing to take bigger risks.

In the summer of 2001, it was a big risk for 20-year-old Hal Elrod to be out selling at all.

Just six weeks earlier, Elrod had been involved in a horrific car accident. His rescuers needed almost an hour to use the Jaws of Life to pry open the top of the car and extract him. The side impact of the crash had broken 13 of Hal's bones and put him in a coma for several days. The doctors had believed that his brain function would never return, and that he would never walk again.

Yet here he was, just six weeks after that accident, begging his parents to drive him to his scheduled appointments for the day.

Elrod had already established a history of amazing accomplishments. At 15, he was hosting his own radio show, *Yo Pal Hal*. At 19, he became a record-breaking sales rep in northern California for Cutco, a $100 million direct marketer of kitchen knives and utensils. He was always motivated to succeed and broke several sales records at the company over the 18 months prior to his accident.

The crash—caused by a drunk driver—affected Elrod's frontal orbital lobe; which is actually the part of the brain that is affected by alcohol. Ironically, because of the accident, Elrod's judgment was impaired in a fashion similar to the way one is when drunk. He was prone to dizzy spells, short-term memory loss, and impaired judgment.

The doctors called his recovery nothing short of a miracle. "I was actually pronounced dead at the scene," recalls Elrod. "[Then when I survived] they said I wouldn't walk or even have normal brain function again, but I beat the odds."

When he was told he could go home, he was elated and confused at the same time. "I was still in a lot of pain, and I didn't know what I was going to do next," Elrod says. He loved his job at Cutco and was anxious to get back to work. He especially loved competition, and Cutco was just entering what it calls a "push period," a two-week sales contest where those at the top of the ranks would be rewarded with a cash prize as well as recognition at a regional conference.

"I really wanted to stand on that stage at the end of the two weeks and accept that champion's trophy, but everyone advised against it."

Everyone, that is, except his sales manager.

"I called Jesse, my manager, and told him that I couldn't make the calls," Elrod remembers. "I told him that I wanted to participate and win, but I was in too much pain, and it was hard to make calls. He knew me and how I was wired, and told me, 'Hal, I completely understand, and I wouldn't blame you a bit for taking it easy, but I believe making a

few calls could be the very best therapy you could do for
yourself.'

"He encouraged me to make five calls to current customers and see how it felt. I did, and on the fourth call I
got an appointment."

Immediately afterward, Elrod felt a surge of confidence.
"I could feel my energy level coming back, so I made several
more calls, and got a few more appointments. I didn't know
how I was going to get *to* those appointments, but I knew
I would find a way."

Since he wasn't in any shape to drive himself, Elrod
pleaded for his parents to drive him where he needed to go.
After convincing them that he would either let them take
him or that he would walk, they realized how important it
was to him, and they agreed to bring him where he needed
to go.

Elrod began selling on the Tuesday of the second week
of the push period, so he only had four actual selling days
in which to compete with all the others in the company.
But in those four days, Elrod sold over $7,000 worth of
merchandise—and was recognized at the regional meeting
in San Jose as the number four seller out of 500 reps in the
building.

"I received a standing ovation as I [walked] onstage with
my cane propping me up," says Elrod. "It was the greatest
feeling of my life."

Today, Elrod has a thriving training and sales coaching
business and helps people of all walks of life to succeed.
"Cutco's Five-Minute Rule has helped me through all sorts
of adversity," he says. "The rule is this: You can be discouraged and negative about a situation for five minutes. After
that, be done with it. Don't dwell on it any more. Put it
aside and move forward. I've always been grateful for my

parents and Cutco for the foundation I needed to break
through my toughest moments, and now I help others to
do the same." More information about Elrod's services are
available at www.yopalhal.com.

TAKEAWAYS

Doing What Others Won't

- **Dominant players take risks, take action, and take the lead—often because others choose not to.** They are bolder, braver, and choose to risk failure over inactivity. They don't sit around wondering "what if"—they ask "why not?"
- **Doers don't have to be smarter, more talented, or have greater resources than the competition.** By virtue of their action, they're already farther ahead than those who do nothing.
- **Attitude is a key to doing anything well.** Sales doers generally have excellent attitudes about themselves, their work, and their eventual success. Without it, work simply becomes an activity without a goal.
- **Generosity, creativity, and persistence can all be characteristics of dominant sales performers who are doers.** By giving away valuable information, creating new opportunities that help others achieve their objectives, or doggedly pursuing a goal or challenge, 800-Pound Gorillas distance themselves ahead of others.
- **It's way more fun to be a doer than a spectator.** Outstanding sales pros believe this wholeheartedly, and their success rates—and those of their clients—are proof positive that it works.

5

BECAUSE THEY LOOK GOOD IN BLUE TIGHTS

Why 800-Pound Gorillas Are Heroes to Those They Serve

In the early 1980s, American households were fascinated with a quirky new kind of comedy-drama on prime time television. It featured a rather ordinary special-ed teacher who discovered a spacesuit that gave him superhero powers. But because the suit's instruction manual was missing, he had to learn how to use the powers by trial and error.

The Greatest American Hero starred William Katt as teacher Ralph Hinkley and was a cult hit from 1981 to 1983. The show's first 25 episodes were the gems; as the show progressed, however—and the plot lines devolved from helping individuals to saving the globe from annihilation— it became less interesting, and ultimately was cancelled after 43 episodes.

The real genius behind the show's early episodes was that it portrayed the attempts by an average person to use the suit's vast powers in an awkward, unsure way. People enjoyed Ralph's average-guy approaches and eventual successes. His attempts at flying, for example, didn't look like the sleek bullet shape of a Superman with arms outstretched in front of him. As Ralph flew, his arms and legs were flailing about, and he seemed unsure of what to do or where to tuck them for maximum flight advantage. In similar fashion, Ralph began to unlock the powers of the suit one by one: resistance to bullets, super strength, invisibility, X-ray vision, and many others. In each episode, Ralph discovered how to use each capability, and then how to use that power to benefit others.

In very much the same way, what separates 800-Pound Gorillas from others in business is their desire and willingness to try every apparatus in their tool belts to be heroes for their customers. As in *The Greatest American Hero* on TV, trial and error is essential in selling, and the ultimate goal for many of selling's dominant players is to constantly figure out the very best way to be a hero to those they serve.

TRIAL, TRIAL AGAIN

Pharmaceutical reps have become a vital link between drug companies and the physicians that prescribe their products to patients. Often, physicians are looking to these experts to let them know what's new and what's in development in new treatments.

Clint Cora is a successful speaker, author, and martial arts expert from the Toronto, Ontario, area (www.clintcora .com). Prior to becoming a speaker, Cora was a very successful pharma rep whose list of clients included Dr. W., a long-time physician who had a huge practice of mainly elderly patients. Cora knew that Dr. W. had been interested in a new drug that his company was producing used to protect elderly patients from stomach ulcers. When the drug finally came out, Cora was pleased to supply Dr. W. with several samples, which the doctor quickly put to the test for himself and three of his best friends—all of whom were of the proper age and at risk for developing stomach ulcers.

Unfortunately, this drug was initially launched with a four-times-per-day dosing schedule. "At this dosage, a significant percentage of patients experienced a nasty side effect," says Cora, "namely, diarrhea."

The next day, after taking the drug, Dr. W. and his three buddies went out to play their favorite game—which was golf. At the ninth hole, all four men suddenly experienced the drug's side effect. Their golf game was certainly cut short.

When Cora revisited Dr. W., he told him the story; and based on his awful experience with the drug, told Cora that he would never prescribe that product again. This was a major setback for Cora, because Dr. W. was one of the most important customers in the entire sales territory. He had a huge practice and many potential patient candidates for the drug.

Dr. W. did, however, like one of the other drugs in Cora's portfolio of products, and so Cora continued to visit the physician in support of the other product. As their relationship continued, Dr. W. grew to trust Cora more and more. He attended one Cora's company's medical education events and learned that top specialists were experiencing great success with the stomach ulcer medication without the diarrhea side effect at a twice-per-day dosage instead of four times daily. At this lower dosage, patients were still adequately protected from stomach ulcers—but without the nasty side effect.

"I encouraged Dr. W. to try the drug out on a few patients at the lower dosage as reported at the medical conference," says Cora. "It took an entire year before Dr. W. did eventually try the drug again." When he did, patients came back reporting good results without side effects.

Dr. W. prescribed the drug to more patients—including himself—again. No side effects were noticed this time. Over the next few months, Dr. W. gave the drug to a huge portion of his elderly patients with great success, and he became one of Cora's biggest supporters in the sales territory.

"I took the time [that I had been given] to build Dr. W.'s trust and provided good service," says Cora. "He was a worst-case scenario but eventually became one of the biggest users of the product, which, of course, eventually helped hundreds of his patients."

LOOKING OUT FOR OTHERS

Heroics in sales involves looking out for the best interests of those you serve, helping them resolve challenges in their lives.

Several years ago, Southern California real estate broker Michael Soon Lee (who we met in Chapter 2) was presented with an ethical challenge. He found himself in the living room of an elderly woman who was interested in listing her home with him. As they spoke, he did some mental calculations and estimated that the home would bring around $350,000 on the current market.

He asked the woman if she had given any thought to what price she would want to ask for the home. "My husband and I bought this house together in 1930 for $18,000," she beamed proudly. "I won't take more than $100,000 for it."

Michael was shocked. "Surely you'd want to ask more if you could get it, wouldn't you?" he replied. She refused.

Recalling that moment, Michael says, "An agent who was only in it for the kill would see this as a golden opportunity. Many people have said I was crazy not to have taken it for $100,000 myself and then selling the house for $350,000 and pocketing a quarter million."

But Michael paused, and thought for a moment. He sensed that there may have been some mental regression in the older woman, and he didn't want her to be a victim. He quickly came up with a plan.

"Okay. I'll agree to list your home for $100,000, but only if two of your relatives agree to the price along with you. If two others from your own family say it's okay, then I'll be glad to do it."

The woman agreed, and asked two family members to assist her. Those two family members saw the state the woman was in, saw the value of the home relative to her own personal valuation, and convinced her to list it at the much higher price. The property sold at $370,000, which was more than enough to pay for the woman's care—which was discovered to be necessary—for the rest of her life.

THE STRONG, SILENT TYPE

Those who perform heroic feats for their customers don't often call themselves heroes. In fact, some 800-Pound

Gorillas try to escape the limelight out of respect for those they serve.

Blair Minton is an unassuming, genteel man who runs an incredibly successful company in a niche that very few others want to touch. Minton is founder and chairman of BMA Management, a company that owns and operates over 30 separate assisted-living residences in Illinois and Indiana. BMA is growing by double digits each year and enjoyed a 28 percent increase in 2008—a year in which no one else in the industry posted *any* growth. It has become the dominant company of its kind in the nation at providing housing for its specific niche: senior citizens with limited means.

"The big players in our business don't want to get into the public aid business," says Minton. Most every other assisted-living company goes after the cream of the crop—the private-pay or market rate residents who make more than $25,000 a year and can afford the housing on their own. BMA, however, has developed a formula that allows poorer people a chance to live in comfortable sur-roundings for 40 percent less than the government would pay for them to be somewhere else.

Occupancy has never been a problem for BMA's residences. While the largest players struggle with 80 to 85 percent occupancy rates, BMA's occupancy rate is above 99 percent. "There are always going to be poor peo-ple," says Minton, matter-of-factly. "Our market segment is growing a lot faster than most others."

Minton's residences are state-licensed as residential care facilities and not as nursing homes, so they have far fewer requirements and reporting mandates. This structure is part of what allows them to operate more efficiently. "We give people with little or no means of supporting themselves a place to live with dignity," says Minton. "We give people their own clean, private place; we treat them with respect; and we give them the ability to live the way they choose."

That passion to provide those less fortunate with something better is what drives Minton and his staff. Minton is motivated in part because of what he saw his own mother go through several years ago as a traditional nursing home resident. "The aides came in to give her a bath at midnight—because that was the only time they had available to do it. She was a slave to their schedule. They didn't care about her. There was no recognition of her as a human being; she was something that they had to deal with." Minton saw it as a problem that desperately needed fixing, and he and his company are doing it one resident at a time.

Although its profit levels may not be as high as its market rate competition, BMA's business is booming, and that kind of volume is creating a healthy cash flow. "If you're 75 years old and female today and your husband dies, there's a 60 percent chance that you'll be immediately thrown into a poverty-level situation," Minton says. "The population is growing faster than we can ever handle ourselves."

Indeed, part of BMA's mission has been to open its books to other larger players to try to convince them to adopt its successful model. "There's way more demand for this housing than we can supply, and we're trying to show our competition how to do it," says Minton. "Unfortunately, we've just not had very many takers."

The bigger players are reluctant to place so much trust in the federal government to fund their ventures. This is also the principal sales hurdle Minton faces when he presents a new project to the attorneys of the banks and bond houses that finance his residences.

"It's my biggest sales challenge, bar none," says Minton. So he uses the following three strategies to sell his projects.

1. The Facts. In 2008, BMA saved the state of Illinois $65 million in public aid as an alternative to paying a nursing home to take care of its residents. "The numbers will only be growing in the future," he claims.

2. The Politics. Minton points out that as the number of disadvantaged people grows in the United States, their voting strength grows, and public aid dollars will be at the forefront of sacred cows that legislators dare not touch for fear of falling out of favor with their constituencies. "AARP is the largest single voting bloc in America and will continue to grow," Minton stresses. "Demand for assisted-living housing in the private-pay sector has all but dried up in 2009, but there is far more demand in our disadvantaged sector, which is more than 60 percent of the senior population and growing."

3. The Human Touch. His most convincing strategy is to show the attorneys the ways in which his product changes lives firsthand. Minton often takes the lawyers and bank executives on a tour of a nearby BMA residence. He shows them where their money is going and tells stories of how lives are being changed as a result of their investment.

One particular bondsman was so moved by BMA's mission that he took Minton aside after the deal had been done. "Blair," he said, "this is the only project we're involved with that I can honestly feel good about when I go to sleep at night."

A highly anticipated annual event is the BMA Bond-holders' Thank-You Gathering, held in Chicago to honor those who are making the company's residences a reality. It's a chance for BMA to retell its positive, life-changing stories, and to reinforce its investors' decisions about their money and the good work it's doing for others.

"People fly in from all over—from New York, California, or wherever they're from—for this meeting," Minton says. "These are really busy people, but they want to hear the stories, what's new, and what's next. We love being able to reward their faith in us like this."

Companies don't necessarily have to have the highest profiles to qualify as 800-Pound Gorillas. Sometimes it's enough to be a hero to those whose voices might never be heard at all.

TAKEAWAYS

Being a Hero to Those You Serve

- **Heroes are those in business whose meaningful actions affect others' lives in a profoundly positive way.** Those who deliver heroic kinds of products or services see their profession not as just a job but as the fulfillment of a much deeper mission.

- **The dominant players in any marketplace are ultimately the ones who are most helpful to others' lives.** Selling is helping, and the 800-Pound Gorillas in any category are primarily the ones who have found ways to help others best, whether measured by price, service, innovation, or any of several other criteria.

♦ **Heroics don't always equate to profitability.** For many dominant players, the mission of the company is not solely driven by financial gain. Many 800-Pound Gorillas could make more money, but choose not to do so because of the reduced impact their product or service would ultimately have on others' lives. By accepting less profit, these dominant players actually ensure their long-term success by providing others the opportunity to win with them, which means more repeat business and more opportunities.

6

THE REALLY STRONG, REALLY SILENT TYPE

How 800-Pound Gorillas Talk Less and Do More

Clutch Cargo was an animated American television series produced by Cambria Studios in the late 1950s and early 1960s. Done on a very limited budget, the show chronicled the adventures of a rugged, handsome pilot (Clutch) accompanied by a young boy (Spinner) and a dachshund mascot (Paddlefoot) as they were sent on dangerous assignments around the world. It was a surprise hit on TV, not just because of its content but because of its creepy "moving-mouth" animation.

Each episode was put together so cheaply that you could barely call it an animated show. The eerie mouths of the characters were practically the only movements at all.

The mouths were actually filmed movements of a human mouth superimposed onto the cartoon character's still picture. The technique, called Syncro-Vox, was invented by Edwin Gillette, part-owner of Cambria at the time. (Conan O'Brien, the late night American TV talk show host, has spoofed this Syncro-Vox technique many times in comedy interview segments with celebrities, using a still picture of the celebrity with only a superimposed mouth moving.)

Creator of the *Clutch Cargo* series Clark Haas claimed that by using Syncro-Vox and other innovative methods of simulating movement, his studio saved hundreds of thousands of dollars in production costs. "Footage that Disney creates for $250,000 we do for $18, 000," he boasted. And the only thing that moved on Clutch Cargo was his mouth.

Do you know any salespeople like that?

There are countless sales reps that talk a good game—but when it's time to make something happen, they always seem to fall short. Something comes up or gets in the way, and while all that is going on, someone who is predisposed to action has already wrapped it up. Perhaps those fast-talking reps ought to be listening to that Toby Keith country song "A Little Less Talk and a Lot More Action" in the car on the way to work.

GUILTY AS CHARGED

As a speaker, an entrepreneur, and a salesman myself, at one point in my career I was just as guilty as anyone else of doing more talking than acting.

When I began my career as a professional speaker in 2003, I was very green and not completely sure of myself. Although I had some programs and topics prepared, I just didn't feel like my overall image was put together and represented correctly. I went to the local chapter meetings of the National Speakers' Association, took careful notes, networked, and did all the right things, but I still felt unfocused.

That's why I took particular notice when a slightly oversized postcard arrived in the mail one day. It featured a friend of mine on one side who had used a speaking career coach name Juanell Teague.

This speaker friend was someone I admired greatly. She was the very first person I met at my first National Speakers' Association convention in New Orleans a few years back, and I can recall how envious I was of how together she appeared. Her platform was rock-solid, her speaking business was thriving, and she had the vision for her own future in the business that I so desperately wanted. If I could just get to her level, I thought, I'd be set.

And that's why I did a complete double-take upon reading her testimonial for Teague's services.

She was quoted on the postcard as saying that Teague had helped her hone and refine her niche, prepare the keynote speech she had always wanted to deliver, and put her on the right track for growth. It was a glowing recommendation for Juanell Teague's services—from someone who I had assumed never needed them!

If Teague can help *her* get even *more* together, I thought, I wonder what she could do for *me*?

I looked over the postcard and I saw that Teague was offering a free 30-minute consultation. But I had more important and pressing things to do—or so I told myself—so I set the postcard aside and did nothing.

About three weeks later, I got the second postcard. It was the same size and format, different photo and complimentary testimonial—but unmistakably Juanell Teague.

I didn't know the person who was featured on this one, but it was equally compelling. It offered the same benefit statements, same free 30-minute offer—and no strings. It had me more interested than ever. But I was still busy. This time, I put the postcard in my "In" box. (That was a step forward.)

Three weeks after that, the third postcard came, with a third testimonial—from someone else with whom I was familiar from the New Orleans convention! I started looking around my office for the hidden cameras. How does she know that I know these people, I wondered? How does she know that they're thinking what I'm thinking?

Hmm, I said to myself. As a salesperson, I need to start taking notes on how she's doing this. Did I want to call? Yes, I did. Did I want to know what magic potions this Juanell lady was putting out? Yes.

But *did* I call?

No. I was chicken. Chicken to expose my flawed business to anyone, chicken to admit that I needed help, and chicken to let anyone in the business know that I couldn't afford the kind of money she charged.

Which is why the next thing she did was so *incredibly* effective.

About two weeks after my third postcard, I got a phone call from someone who was making phone appointments on behalf of Juanell Teague.

"I'm calling from Juanell Teague's office," the young lady said sweetly. "Juanell has looked at your web site, done some research, and identified you as a speaker she would very much like to work with. She's very choosy about whom she selects, and she has asked me to call you to set up a free, no-obligation conference call."

Her voice drifted off inside my head.

I was being sold! I was being *set up* for being sold! It was so eloquent, so predictable, so . . . *good*—and I couldn't help myself.

"Would you be available a week from Thursday at. . . " the sweet young lady sang to me.

Must. . . Resist. . . . . must. . . . . resist. . . . . .

Oh, it's pointless to fight it! It's *free!*

"Yes," I replied calmly. "Next Thursday would be fine."

CAUGHT UP IN A SALES FUNNEL

Juanell Teague is a doer; she's someone who has created a sustainable system of lead generation and cultivation that eventually leads her potential clients to the logical conclusion that she is the best one for the job. Her sales funnel—or process of systematically bringing her prospects to the logical conclusion of utilizing her services—is brilliant.

How exactly does this sales funnel work to help Teague sell her services? Let's take a closer look at the elements of her approach with me:

1. **She prequalified me.** She saw that I was a member of my trade association (the National Speakers' Association); did some homework on me by looking at my web site, my materials, and where I was in my career; and selected me as someone she wanted to target. She didn't pick everyone in NSA, just those in whom she saw an opportunity to help. If I hadn't fit the criteria—a speaker with a good start and a need for professional direction—I wouldn't have made the list of prospects.

2. **She established familiarity with me first.** She created multiple postcards with her picture on them and sent them, knowing it would take more than one impression to make the initial "credibility sale." She knew that they might not last long on my desk; but she also knew I would at least read them before I tossed them away, which would leave a mental impression upon which she would capitalize later.

3. **She used testimonials on the postcards that I could relate to.** She had no idea that I knew two of the three people she featured, but they spoke directly to me and where I was in my career. They had the same issues, the same challenges, the same pain; and each one had been helped by Teague in the same way. It was powerful proof of her ability to get the job done.

4. **She spaced out multiple communications with me over a period of weeks.** Every three weeks or so, I got a new and unique postcard. Each one brought me closer to the decision stage, even though none of them directly resulted in a phone call. (That's an important point; just because I didn't pick up the phone doesn't mean it wasn't effective in creating an impression.)

5. **She didn't rely on her marketing to move me to action.** She reached out by phone to set up the initial appointment—something I may or may not have done on my own.

6. **She sold me a low-risk proposition first.** By agreeing to the 30-minute consultation, I was under no obligation to buy anything. In a half hour of talking about me and my situation, I thought I might

learn something valuable about what next steps I needed to take. The choice to continue and invest would be completely mine.

7. **She had someone else make the appointment for her.** Her assistant made the call, giving me a positive impression of the value of her time. It also set up something of a mystique surrounding finally getting to talk to Teague herself on the appointed day. By letting someone else set it up, she actually increased the perceived value of our 30-minute consultation.

These are the actions of an 800-Pound Gorilla at its finest.

Prior to our 30-minute conversation, Teague sent me an e-mail with a brief questionnaire attached. It inquired about my previous speaking engagements, what I was currently doing, and what I wanted to be doing in the business. She asked me to complete it prior to our call so she could read through my information, formulate her questions more carefully, and get quickly to the heart of her phone conversation with me.

Many other 800-Pound Gorillas use this strategy very effectively. They either dig up the information themselves, or have the prospects supply it for them. For example, at ActionCoach Canada, a franchisor and provider of career coaching services, Greg Kopchuk prequalifies those who show interest in becoming a business coaching client of the company by asking them to fill out a brief questionnaire, either by hand or online.

"The questionnaire is a must before I'll go to see someone," Kopchuk explains. "It asks them specific things about what's going on in their business, and gets the business owner to think in the right ways before we even walk in the door."

Rather than just giving it out, however, Kopchuk suggests letting the prospect know *why* it would be in their best interest to fill it out. "If you explain the reasons why a client should fill it out, they're much more receptive to the process, rather than simply handing them the paperwork or giving out the Web address."

Once he gets the completed questionnaire, Kopchuk calls the prospect to review what's going on in that individual's business, just to make sure he or she sees value in the upcoming meeting. "After filling it out, the prospect is usually looking forward to our get-together," he says.

IT'S ALL ABOUT THE DOING

Jeb Blount is a doer. He's just not a very good "no"-sayer.

"I hate to not help people. I just tell everybody that it's okay, and that I'll do whatever they ask," says Blount. "I get burned every now and then, but not very often. And when I decide to get something done, I move really fast. I take action."

Blount is the creator and starship commander of SalesGravy.com, the most-visited sales content site on the Internet. SalesGravy.com has more than 400,000 visitors, 3 million page views, and 10 million hits every single month. "In February of '09, we had an average of 35 page views per visitor," says Blount. "Think about that. That's huge. Do you know how much content is on 35 pages? That means people are searching around for hours on our site and reading page after page of great stuff. It's become one of the top 20,000 web sites out of the 10 million web sites in the world."

Blount began SalesGravy with a few friends in January of 2007. "We just got it going and tried to break stuff," Blount recalls. "We jumped in and got our hands dirty. We experimented, looked at the data, and experimented again. We keep tinkering and improving the product to the point where we know now what works and what doesn't. We've changed almost 100 percent of the site from where we started. The only thing that's still there from our first day online is the banner on the top of the page."

Blount's sales career started at age 23, when he sold nutrition and counseling programs for NutriSystem Weight Loss Centers. "I was good because I *did* stuff. I listened to people. I wasn't as interested about selling them a program as I was figuring out why they wanted the results we provided," recalls Blount.

Shortly after becoming the number one salesperson in the area, Blount set his sights on becoming the district manager of several centers. His area manager, however, was unconvinced he could do it. "She came down to my center and put me to the test. She said, 'Pick someone out of the lobby of the building, bring her in here, give her the tour, and if you sell her, I'll consider you for the DM job.' I picked out a random woman who just happened to be in the lobby, gave her the facility tour, asked her a few questions, and listened to her. I told her a little bit about NutriSystem, and when I was done, she started writing me a check for our Premier program— the highest-priced program we offered—before I could even tell her how much the program was!"

Yes—he got the district manager job.

SalesGravy.com is a huge extension of Jeb Blount the salesperson. "I have an ability to help others make emotional connections between things, then relate it to something they know and help them to understand the connections." And that's exactly what SalesGravy.com does extremely well. It's part education, part Facebook, part coffee shop. People come to learn, exchange, and grow in their field of professional sales. The hundreds of posted articles are from recognized experts in selling, and the content is all free. "I love the whole business of aggregating training and sales into one place," he says.

There's no slowing Blount down with meaningless conversation about doing something "someday."

"If somebody's got an idea that makes sense and they bring it to me, I usually say, 'Let's go!' There's no need to waste time thinking about it," says Blount. "I get excited about innovation and new ideas, and I'm ready to go. If somebody says, 'I need to think about it,' I know there's going to be a problem. I'm a believer in trying things and seeing what works. Make a bunch of mistakes. Get in there and do something. Just be flexible. If it isn't working, try it a different way. Just do something."

TAKEAWAYS

Talking Less and Doing More

♦ **Dominant players talk less and take action more than others.** This doesn't mean that they don't take time to carefully plan their activities; it simply means they're predisposed to action vs. standing still.

♦ **800-Pound Gorillas use systems to get more out of every action they pursue in selling.** Acting impulsively is often not a smart business move. The best sales professionals use systems that are carefully designed to guide a prospect through the different phases of the product's discovery, education, desire, and call to action. Each effort is there to move the prospect to the next phase, in logical sequence. That way, each expenditure of effort is placed just where it needs to be. The less time that is spent on wasted effort, the more return that can be realized per hour.

◆ **In an 800-Pound Gorilla's world, doing something and making a mistake is far better than talking about potentially making a mistake.** Those who are dominant players believe that with action there is information, learning, and progress taking place. "Analysis paralysis," or talking about action incessantly without doing anything, drives them crazy.

7

ONE BANANA, TWO BANANA

How 800-Pound Gorillas Add Value

There are people the world over who enjoy fishing as a sport. And then there are fly fishermen.

For generations, the purpose of fishing was to provide sustenance and prolong survival; it wasn't done as a sport. But today, the art of fly fishing is highly revered in many parts of the world. The careful tying and preparing of the flies and the gear, the one-with-nature feeling of the surroundings, the wading into a moving stream, the study and mimicking of the real insects and their water-landing patterns, and the thrill of hooking a brook trout or salmon are indescribable experiences to those who enjoy the sport.

Fly fishermen use different flies at different times of the year to mimic the current stages of the local insect population. They alter casting techniques—throwing the line just right to place the fly on top of the water—depending on the type of fish, the water's current, the wind, the fly being used, and the temperature. They explore various spots along the rivers and streams at different stages of the season, all the while remaining very respectful of the environment.

"Just fishing?" Don't ever say that to a fly fisherman. It's nature, art, lifestyle, and religion all rolled into one. And the 800-Pound Gorilla of fly fishing is Orvis.

The Orvis Company, headquartered in Manchester, Vermont, and founded in 1856, is the nation's oldest mail-order company. Charles Orvis—a native of Vermont and an avid fly fisherman—produced and patented the first ventilated narrow-spool fly fishing reel in 1874. According to the book, *The Orvis Story*, Orvis rods, reels, and hand-tied flies became widely recognized as well-made, reliable, and fairly priced.

Today, The Orvis Company is a privately held mega-brand that boasts a blend of mail-order and retail businesses, guided fishing and hunting trips, and several fly-fishing and shooting schools in the United States and the United Kingdom. The company web site (www.orvis.com) claims that fishing gear accounts for about 25 percent of its total sales. The company doesn't regularly disclose annual sales figures, but *Vermont Business* magazine reported its 2006 sales at $280 million.

Company President Leigh Perkins, Jr., gives us a glimpse of why Orvis has grown to become the dominant fish in the pond. In a 2006 interview (www.allbusiness .com/sales/1136645-1.html), Perkins explained: "We sell a lifestyle and experience, not just a product line. We're helping people who want to enjoy being outdoors."

Orvis has extended into selling fishing properties with lakes on them and lifestyle villages with natural hunting and fishing resources. "It's like a golf village community, but for fishing or other natural pursuits instead," says Perkins. The company has seen that in creating the resources to enjoy the sport, it's also promoting the use of its brand.

Ask anyone who's into fly fishing about quality products, and the name Orvis will be the first that gets mentioned. Do the same with driving, and no doubt BMW will be at the top of the list.

The German automaker has built its brand around the tagline, "The Ultimate Driving Machine." Most BMW enthusiasts in the United States are passionate about their vehicles; however, they don't have the opportunity to put their machines through their paces quite like the twists and turns they see in the TV commercials. BMW, like Orvis, has chosen to expand its influence on the customer to include a deeper and broader experience.

The BMW Performance Center—located just outside Greenville, South Carolina—is a $12 million drivers' paradise. Built in 1999, it is home to the BMW Performance Driving School, where drivers can immerse themselves—along with a team of high-level driving experts—in learning how to extract the highest level of performance out of their vehicles. As the company's web site (www.relearntodrive.com) states, "BMW ownership is not required; a passion for driving is."

The two-mile test track includes a spectrum of challenges, educational opportunities, and of course, plenty of competitive races with fellow students that cover everything from gravel and stone to wet surfaces, cones, road courses, ovals, and defensive maneuvering techniques. Students all drive brand-new BMWs—from the nimble

M Coupe to the brute-like 507-horsepower M5—which reinforces the brand and promotes the features of the new models very effectively. If you kicked butt with a new Beamer in this school, you won't settle for anything less when you get back home.

A recent BMW sales promotion included a one-day Driving School experience for two at no additional cost. A $1,300 value, BMW even picks up the tab for your hotel and meals.

It isn't enough to say its vehicles are The Ultimate Driving Experience. BMW has added value to its brand by actually helping you figure out how it's done.

MONEY CAN BE NO OBJECT ... BUT MOST TIMES, IT IS

Wal-Mart has long been the 800-Pound Gorilla of retail and has managed to attain that status using a single differentiator: price. So where can others add value in a world that screams "low prices"?

Perhaps no one does value-added—or, in its own words, "Wow!"—better than Zappos.com, an online retailer of shoes, clothing, handbags, and more. Based near Las Vegas in Henderson, Nevada, Zappos' 2008 gross sales topped $1 billion; a 15 percent increase from 2007. Using current estimates of online footwear sales, Zappos easily commands 30 percent of the market—an 800-Pound Gorilla if there ever was one. (Amazon.com agreed to buy Zappos.com Inc. for approximately $890 million in July of 2009, and the deal was expected to close by the end of the year.)

Founded in 1999 by Nick Swimmurn after a frustrating search for shoes in a San Francisco mall, Zappos' entire business model is predicated on adding value in one fundamental category: customer service. The company's value proposition? Buy from us, and our amazingly friendly people will take your order and ship it lightning-fast for free. If you don't like what you order, send it back within a year—for free—and we'll give you a full refund. Our selection is so big, though, that you're almost guaranteed to find something else you like.

"Eventually, we want to be selling anything and everything with overnight shipping," says Zappos' CEO Tony Hseih. "We're listening to our customers and finding out what it is they'd like us to sell; that's what has led us to begin selling electronics and housewares. If our customers asked us to start an airline—which a few already have—we might seriously consider that in the future."

What has developed is a "product-agnostic" business model, according to Zappos' Business Development Specialist Aaron Magness. "We consider ourselves a service company, first and foremost. We just happen to drive our service model with shoes, but it could be anything; and at some point down the road, it *will* be anything and everything that makes sense for us to sell. Our customers will dictate that for us."

On any given day, 75 percent of Zappos' orders are from repeat customers. "We encourage all of our Customer Loyalty Team members to form personal connections with our customers," says Magness. "That builds word-of-mouth marketing, which we think is much better than traditional media advertising to build our business."

During a recent phone order, a Zappos rep learned that the customer was nursing a badly sprained ankle. After the order was placed, the rep grabbed a blank Zappos note card, wrote a little get well message, had 10 others around her sign it, and sent it in the mail to the customer. "The customer was blown away," says Magness.

"Nobody else does that kind of thing—especially not as big a company as we are." That customer blogged about her Zappos experience—and even scanned the get well card to show others what she had received. "You can't buy word-of-mouth like that. That's why we do what we do. Yes, it's more time-consuming, and it's a leap of faith on our part, but it's so rare in business today, the end result is almost predictable." Magness estimates that 10 percent of the orders that go out are accompanied by a little note card sent separately through the U.S. mail.

Each team member is rated on a much different scale than that used by most call centers. "We don't measure number of calls, call times, average order size, cross-sell, up-sell, or any of those things," Magness beams. "We measure our people on one thing: Did you WOW! the customer? If they each do that, we've done our job; everything else will flow from there."

Zappos does spend money on traditional advertising, but it's minimal. The company's media buy for 2009 was a grand total of $3 million—a paltry sum compared to its sales figures. "We consider the money spent on note cards and postage part of our marketing budget," says Magness. "The free shipping we offer, the generous return policy, the extra time we spend with people on the phones—all these things take time and money, which we consider part of our marketing effort."

But does the company give their customers low prices and great deals? Isn't that what consumers are begging for?

Zappos has taken a decidedly different stand. "We charge nearly full price for most of the items we sell," says Magness. "Price-sensitive customers are not the most loyal customers. What we've found matters to our customers is not the final price tag, but the brand of service we provide. They're actually willing to pay the price for what they know they'll receive."

In the beginning, Zappos drop-shipped much of its inventory through other vendors. However, that led to a lack of management oversight. "If one of our vendors had a computer problem or had a truck that broke down, we couldn't control that, and it made us look bad," explains Magness. "We had a team-wide meeting in 2003 to figure out what our company was going to be when it grows up. We had a lot of discussion, and we decided that we didn't necessarily want to be the biggest shoe retailer in the world. Instead, we wanted to continue to build a company culture that put customers first. It then became obvious that we needed to control all of the aspects of the service our customers received. Once we made that decision, all the other decisions were a lot easier."

After that meeting, Zappos set out to build its own warehouse distribution center in Kentucky so that it could control the shipping itself. "It's a much more expensive route to take than simply acting as a third-party seller and letting someone else do the fulfillment, but it's absolutely the best option for the customer," says Magness. "We run our center in Kentucky 24 hours a day, so if someone in New York orders a pair of shoes online at midnight, we can literally have those shoes at her doorstep at 8 A.M."

Wow.

PRICE ... VALUE ... HOW DO YOU FEEL ABOUT IT?

Most Zappos customers aren't price-shopping; if they were, they'd buy from someone else. Zappos makes no apologies for selling at full price, because it knows its customers value the service it provides first and foremost. As a salesperson, how do you feel about what you charge for your wares?

If the price of your product or service is a problem for you personally, it's very likely to also be an issue for your customers. However, 800-Pound Gorillas have mastered the art of using price as an effective lever to build a higher perceived value in the minds of their prospects.

Barry Maher knows this as well as anyone. As one of the most successful Yellow Pages advertising sales reps in the world for GTE Directories, Maher sold twice as much product annually as his closest rival at GTE for four years running. *TIME* magazine called him, "By far, the leading expert on the subject." And one of Maher's secrets to becoming an 800-Pound Gorilla is his dramatic use of the product's price during his presentations.

"Before a presentation, a prospect would ask me how much my Yellow Pages program costs," says Maher, "and I would say, 'It's a boatload! It's *very* expensive! And here's the reason why it's worth every penny.' I would then present all the benefits of the advertising—the testimonials, the business growth statistics, all the evidence of the product's value."

According to Maher, a very interesting thing would then happen. "After my compelling value presentation—when I finally got to the price of the advertising—my customers were surprised that it was actually *lower* than they were expecting. The value of my product was obvious for the price I was asking, and many bought on the spot."

Maher cleverly (and ethically!) established the product's extensive value up front—and when value and cost were put side-by-side on the table, the decision became an easy one for the client.

VALUE IS MORE THAN MONEY

Although Barry Maher's lever is heavily price-driven, some customers want more than a good product at a fair price; they need someone to help them navigate the use of the product or service so they can best utilize it to their advantage.

Brad White is vice president of sales for AddVenture Products (www.addv.com), a manufacturer and distributor of printed advertising specialty items. The company's bread-and-butter item is a specialized compressed T-shirt that can be shaped in any of hundreds of ways to form a unique logo giveaway. In an industry where a company that does $1 million in sales volume is the general measure of success, White has personally sold multiple millions each year—and is one of the largest volume sellers in his industry.

AddVenture sells its products through a worldwide network of advertising specialty distributors that can select from among several vendors for the products they sell to end users. To differentiate his company from others that offer similar products, White has found success by positioning himself as a partner rather than a vendor.

"My ultimate goal is to have all the distributors sell my stuff and no one else's," admits White. "There are several ways to do that; but I believe the most effective way is to be the most valuable vendor to the customer."

Value takes many forms, but in White's cutthroat world of advertising specialties, he has become an 800-Pound Gorilla by creating opportunities for his partners to make money.

"Our signature T-shirt product is screen printed and then squeezed into a shrink-wrapped shape of whatever you want. There are hundreds of options—round, square, logo-shaped; whatever shape you want to create," explains White. "I can't expect each of my dozens of partners to know all of the cool applications my product can fulfill; each of them has hundreds of products to learn. Knowing that, I've decided that for everyone's sake, I need to work much more closely with my distributor/partners than most people in my industry are used to."

Each call White receives from a distributor or partner is handled much differently than the callers have come to expect with other vendors. "These guys are used to people that are taking T-shirt orders. I want to work with them as a marketer—to help them see the potential of the product, and to look beyond the product itself. If we can all work together to get the most out of every opportunity, then everybody benefits—the vendor, his customer, the customer's eventual end user, and certainly us."

Though this kind of approach takes longer, White claims that it is infinitely more valuable to everyone involved. "Initially, I'll ask them, 'What does the eventual buyer of the product want to achieve with this T-shirt? What's the goal of the purchase? What does it mean to the eventual recipient of the item? What does the buyer want the end user to do, feel, or experience as a result of having this item?' These are the kinds of questions that many in our industry just may not think to ask but are critical to the project's success."

The end result may be much different from what the buyer was originally seeking, but in White's view, that's a good thing. "It means the customer got what he really needed rather than what he *thought* he wanted," says White. "There's a huge difference."

Case in point: A major brewery came to one of White's distributors knowing what it wanted but not quite sure of what it needed. "They had created an opportunity to hold an instant-win contest," White explains. "They wanted to give away a total of four week-long vacations for four to a private island destination and do it in a unique way. The distributor thought it might be something our company could help with, and since we had worked together on some other projects, he and I began working as a team to solve this for the client." White learned that the campaign's goal was to move buyers of 6-packs of the product up to the 12-pack using the instant-win incentive inside the larger package. Even if buyers didn't win the trip, however, the brewer wanted the in-pack incentive to have value to each person who received it rather than just being something that would be thrown away. The client also wanted the item to identify the brand longer-term—such as would happen with wearing a T-shirt—which is what led the distributor to call White.

"We brainstormed the project, and eventually created a dynamite program for the client: a printed T-shirt that was compressed to look like the unique bottle shape of the brand and that would fit inside the center of a 12-pack of 12-ounce bottles," says White. "It was shrink-wrapped with a paper insert that described what was inside the package and explained that four lucky winners would find a voucher for a trip for four to the private island."

The brewer loved White's concept. It placed an order for 500,000 compressed T-shirts, and the promotion was a huge success. "The giveaway created enormous buzz, their 12-pack sales increased dramatically, and their brand was everywhere," says White. "We helped them achieve their goal, and we achieved ours in the process."

To prepare for a sales call, AddVenture's Brad White uses the acronym A-V-G, which stands for "average" in baseball. The three letters represent the three things he considers prior to a sales call:

Audience. White does his homework prior to the call, whether it's on the phone or in person. "Web sites are great because that's where a company will tell you who they want you to think they are," White says. "You'll learn what's important to them on their site. You'll learn who the company officers are, where their locations are, their range of products or services, and other relevant bits of information that you'll need to know during the sales call."

Value. This is where White assesses what he brings to the table personally, and how it adds to the potential equation. "Where is my value to them? How can I benefit them and be aware of it so I can bring it up at the right time in our conversation?"

Goal. "What is my goal in this sales call, and how can I look for potential common goals between me and my contact so that we can achieve some results together?" asks White. "By being aware of my goal at all times, my communications are more valuable; they're not just open-ended, but they lead to a point."

TAKEAWAYS

Adding Value

♦ **Adding value beyond price is a fundamental practice of almost every 800-Pound Gorilla.** In addition to the product or service provided for the money, often there is something deeper and more profound that is exchanged when an 800-Pound Gorilla is involved.

♦ **Value means different things to different people.** Although sometimes equated with money, what's valuable to one person may not be at all valuable to another. Items or actions of value that 800-Pound Gorillas deliver successfully may include things like superior service, creative ideas, the feelings about a particular brand, or over-and-above partnerships with shared risk. The important thing is that the item or action must be seen as valuable to the *customer*—regardless of the giver's perceived value.

♦ **The positioning of value relative to price can be critical in establishing good feelings about the value delivered.** By effectively managing the perceived value of what you sell, you can manage the customer's 'delight factor' relative to your product or service. Help your customers understand what a great value they're getting, and you'll have more customers.

♦ **The more exclusive you can make your added value, the more dominant you can become.** If your product or service is the only one that can deliver on a certain value proposition, you have the potential to be an 800-Pound Gorilla.

8

ROARRRRRR!

Why 800-Pound Gorillas Are the Ones Others Quote

Ozzy Osbourne is not your typical spokesperson. But then again, very few people are as memorable as Ozzy Osbourne.

The English rock artist and current TV icon started his career in the late 1970s fronting the heavy metal band Black Sabbath. His piercing, unmistakable voice ushered in a new era of popularity for heavy metal, and the band's dark, evil-tinged lyrics earned Osbourne the title of "Prince of Darkness."

Osbourne's heavy substance abuse led to his being kicked out of Black Sabbath, and his drug and alcohol problems would follow him for the better part of his career. He recorded several solo albums—a period during which many of his most popular songs were created—and has since reunited with Black Sabbath off and on for live performances for the past 30 years.

Throughout his career, however, Osbourne has been accused of deliberately inciting young people to worship demons and commit horrific acts because of the content of his song lyrics. A litany of lawsuits has been brought against Osbourne, beginning in 1986 with the parents of two boys who committed suicide after listening to the song, "Suicide Solution." Osbourne has denied all of his outrageous stage acts were to glorify Satanism—including alleged portrayals of the devil's "horned hand"—claiming they were done to symbolize teen rebellion and to add "shock value" to his performances.

The strangest part of Osbourne's career, however, has been his success as a TV reality show participant. MTV produced the first episodes of the groundbreaking show *The Osbournes*—which provided a look inside the lives of Ozzy, wife Sharon, and their two teenage children in 2002. It was a shocking, foul-mouthed barrage of everyday defiant behavior, obsessive-compulsive activity, and lapses in normal brain function. Ozzy and Sharon became cult icons in an entirely different way, with each week's show creating a new high—or low—in bizarre behavior.

Despite the illegal activity, bad language, and heavy metal—or perhaps *because* of it—Ozzy Osbourne is one of the most recognized pop figures on the planet. His appearances on several TV commercials, parodying his quotable lines, have become classics in themselves:

"I've been the Price of Darkness since 1979!"

"Sharon!" (yelling loudly, as he was prone to do in many of his reality shows from home) "Mmfmtrblt." (mumbling so badly that no one can understand).

Even today, Ozzy continues to make defiant statements about himself and the world he inhabits through his lyrics. His 2007 platinum-selling album, "Black Rain"—his ninth studio album and the first he claims that was recorded without drugs or alcohol—contains lyrics that defy authority and glorify being high, reckless, and "over the top". This kind of defiant, individualistic attitude is part of what young people find appealing in Ozzy Osbourne. He sings about the same things that they are thinking, and his lyrics then become something that others quote.

Fortunately for you, Mr. or Ms. Salesperson, you don't have to resort to notoriously Ozzy-esque antics like biting the heads off live bats onstage to become quotable. (Ozzy claims the bat was dead, but it's still pretty gross to even think about.)

Being quotable in sales means that your expertise is so highly thought of, your command of the language is so eloquent, your words are so memorable, or your thoughts are so well organized, that someone other than your spouse or your mother was impressed enough to repeat your words verbatim to someone else. Those who are quoted are often considered among the most dominant and influential thinkers of their industry.

So—who's quoting *you*?

EVERY INDUSTRY HAS ITS VOICES

There's a quotable 800-Pound Gorilla in broadcast advertising sales, and his name is Dave Gifford.

"When I was a youngster, one of my teachers predicted I would either be a teacher, a preacher, or a salesman," Gifford recalls. "I became all three."

As a sales and management consultant specializing in teaching commercial broadcast radio companies, managers, and salespeople how to make more money, Gifford has sold millions of dollars in broadcast advertising, and is a member of the prestigious Marquis' *Who's Who in Advertising*. He has practiced what he preaches in his 50-plus-year career in broadcasting, which includes stints at some of the most highly revered broadcast properties in the world. He's a prolific article writer and has been published in several key industry publications. He has a wealth of experience as a salesperson, sales manager, general manager, managing partner, and consultant in 18 countries around the world.

If there's one thing that Gifford has done exceptionally well, it has been to create short, memorable, and meaningful quotes. His observations and insights on what succeeds in broadcast advertising sales have inspired thousands of reps in every corner of the globe. He's a speak-it-like-he-sees-it, snap-you-into-shape, no-holds-barred, doesn't-care-who-he-pisses-off kind of industry leader, and because of this, some people in the radio business don't care for him very much.

"I don't sugarcoat things, and a lot of people don't like that," Gifford says matter-of-factly. He refuses to feed people pablum and contends that nobody remembers back-pedaling and weakly-worded arguments. He thoroughly researches his points, applies his own thoughts developed from half a century of keeping his finger on the pulse of the industry, and he lets 'er rip, critics be damned.

You want to sell more? *"Ask and you get; don't and you won't."* That's Giff's advice: easy to remember, direct, and very quotable. You're in a sales slump? *"There's only three reasons for a slump: personal problems, extenuating circumstances, or too few presentations . . . and there's not a single sales problem in the world that can't be cured by more presentations, more presentations, and more presentations!"* Giff's take on closing: *"Selling is helping, and helping is closing."* And on habits: *"Winners form habits . . . habits form losers!"*

He says the following about sales behaviors: *"Attitude dictates behavior."*

Impossible goals? *"Salespeople are experts in what cannot be done!"*

Don't like doing call reports? Giff says to do them. Why? *"Unseen is unsold is untold."*

You're an advertiser that wants results? *"What you say times how many times you say it is the only thing that works in advertising today. . . and what you say times how many times you say it is the only thing that works in radio today!"*

Wondering if you're going to make it? *"You can succeed because you can't help yourself . . . or you'll fail because you didn't help yourself."*

Here's a few more of Giff's wise quotes on success in selling, along with his logic for each of them, in his own words:

---

1. My father's advice to me as a teenager: "Don't believe everything you read in the newspaper. Much of it is non-sense."

It was a guiding principle that I later converted into an instructional quote: "Argue with the author!"

(AUTHOR'S NOTE: A common theme of quoted individuals or companies—including Gifford—is this kind of contrarian thinking. If you agree with everyone and everything, no one will believe you have an opinion of your own worth quoting.)

2. "Know what you're talking about!"

Consequently, in whatever field you're employed, you need to become a "forever scholar" with a well-honed, built-in BS detector. For example—beside the fact that none of the companies featured in Tom Peters' 1980 best seller *In Search of Excellence* came close to that standard—why do you think TQM (Total Quality Management) and reengineering, former corporate deities, experienced such a short shelf life? Obviously, there were fundamental flaws in their recipes.

3. "If you lack experience you lack knowledge, and to lack knowledge is to lack judgment."

Example: What kind of managers are we currently developing for Fortune 500 companies? It is my conviction—despite the staggering informational yield accumulated through advanced technologies—that we are reaching a point where future CEOs may share a balance of experience, knowledge, and judgment deficient of the standard set by their predecessors in decades past. What is missing? Surprisingly, experience—real, tactile, projectable experiences—plural.

Problem: Young managers today gain most of their experience by working within project teams in a multilayered "filtering" progression on floors below the executive levels. The result—as they work their way through the ranks—is that their acquired knowledge has not been expanded through their own personal experience but has come rather from the input of team members, some of whom proffered widely conflicting opinions.

Is it not a plausible possibility that today's emerging Fortune 500 CEOs—so lacking in field-tested, hands-on experience—have reason to become suspicious of recommendations from subordinates overly influenced by the same imprecise decision making process they were a part of? As a result, they end up tortured by indecision and procrastination. And the consequence may very well be that we are finding ourselves at the precipice of developing a generation of CEOs unable to make crucial decisions fast enough to respond to competitors executing less labored decision making methodologies.

Threat: If we are to compete globally, that prospect should evoke concern in boardrooms across America.

4. "SWOT, not!"

SWOT analysis—credited to Albert Humphrey at Stanford University (using data from Fortune 500 companies for a research project in the 1960s and 1970s)—was initially and primarily used as a strategic planning tool to identify key internal and external factors to achieve a specific objective. Today, however, SWOT is more often *misused* for solving all manner of problems through an analysis of a given company's strengths, weaknesses, threats, and opportunities in that order. And as such this tool has been transformed into one of the most useless problem-solving formulas in the history of business management.

To illustrate: let's say that your company is not growing, and that you are personally held responsible for its top line. Are you going to solve your revenue problems by addressing your strengths first? Ridiculous! You would be wiser, would you not, to start with the threats; next, check out what additional strengths you need to eliminate those weaknesses; and finally—explore those emerging opportunities that have resulted from the reordering of the SWOT analysis sequence. SWOT not; TWSO instead!

5. *"All* company problems are *management* problems!"

Let's say that Company A, having reached a point of zero growth, just embarked on an exhaustive and hugely expensive survey to ascertain the perceptions customers have of their company. Owing to the fact management is not close enough to its customers to know what the company's perception is, Company A obviously has a management problem—true or false? The DNA of a company is the DNA of its CEO.

Controversial or not, one of the hallmarks of Giff's success is the frequency with which he is quoted in the industry. "As a speaker, writer, trainer, and seller," he says, "whatever success I have been fortunate enough to achieve has been totally dependent on which words I chose, the order in which I place those words (the juxtaposition of one word to the next to trigger a positive response), and how I say those words."

EMOTIONAL VOLTAGE

Giff would agree with ad man extraordinaire Roy Williams of Buda, Texas—one of the country's truly great copywriters, thinkers, and philosophers—on the art of modern marketing. Among his well-known quotes is the following: *"The words we use are electric, and should be measured by the emotional voltage they carry."*

If that's true, then the dominant players in sales—the 800-Pound Gorillas—are the virtual power plants of the selling profession.

Is there a phrase of yours that others hear and instantly identify you as the source?

Here are a few notable sayings that are attributed to a single individual. See if you can guess who:

"It's made in Germany. You know, the Germans always make good stuff."

"Are you getting this, camera guy?"

"We can't do this all day."

"Stop having a boring tuna; stop having a boring life."

"You're gonna love my nuts."

"This onion is making you cry, it's making me cry. Life's hard enough as it is, you don't want to cry any more."

"We're gonna make America skinny again . . . one slap at a time."

"Tacos . . . fettuccini . . . linguini . . . martini . . . bikini."

These are all near-legendary phrases from a TV pitchman named Vince Offer Shlomi, better known as "Vince, the ShamWow Guy." Shlomi's product, ShamWow, is a German-made chamois towel with exceptional absorbing qualities, as demonstrated in his infomercial. He also owns and tele-promotes another kitchen item, the Slap Chop, a multiblade food chopping device.

ShamWow won the CNBC.com "As Seen on TV" competition in January 2009 as the best TV-advertised product of all time. More than 300,000 votes were cast on the CNBC web site over an 11-day period, and ShamWow beat initial front-runners like the George Foreman Grill, The Clapper on-off device for household appliances, and the *Girls Gone Wild* series of videos.

In fact, the product won despite the fact that his TV demo has been called into question. In one ShamWow scene, Shlomi pours a volume of cola from a 2-liter bottle onto a carpet square and picks up the wet square to show the drippy mess underneath. The next scene shows him taking the chamois and applying it to the carpet, absorbing the cola stain—and, magically, all the cola underneath the carpet square is gone as well! Until, that is, you look closely—and see that the small puddle that was underneath the carpet magically disappears when the scene changes.

Even with this obvious evidence, many thousands of people remained unfazed and continue to buy the product. Why? How is it that so many people buy Shlomi's chamois, and his follow-up product, the Slap Chop? What goes into becoming the 800-Pound Gorilla of "As Seen on TV" products?

- **He's interesting to listen to.** When Shlomi speaks, people just seem to pay attention. His accent—a combination of Midwest honesty and New York bravado—has a fun, mesmerizing quality that consumers enjoy. His unique lines seem to come from out of nowhere; and they're funny, edgy, and above all else, persuasive.

- **He has several unique characteristics.** One of them is the slightly annoying microphone attached to his head, which is a little unusual—seeing as you don't need one of those on TV. But when you learn Shlomi's story, it makes sense. Part of Shlomi's resume involves selling kitchen utensils at swap meets, using a hands-free microphone to hawk his wares while giving demonstrations. With the microphone in place, it gives the impression that you're *at* the swap meet, watching his high-energy demo and mile-a-minute pitch. It makes him unique among his TV contemporaries; and potentially, a little more believable.

- **He talks as if you'd be crazy not to own his product.** "Sales" is often defined as a transfer of belief from one party to another. With Vince Shlomi, you have no doubt as to whether or not he believes his product is worth every penny.

♦ **He uses the language of everyday Americans.** He says things like "gonna," "look at dis," and "dere y'go" in a way that endears himself to people. He talks like he's your next-door neighbor selling you his lawn mower, only faster—and his hands never stop moving. (Okay, maybe your neighbor's hands don't stop moving either, but that's different.)

♦ **He's a little bit aggressive.** People don't like to be sold, but they love to buy from Shlomi. He's not ashamed to ask for the order, especially when his demo is so darned convincing. "I've been to those flea markets, and nice doesn't get people to stop," said Shlomi in an interview on CNBC after his infomercial's award. "People stop when you are aggressive and you bring people in." (www.cnbc.com/id/28880253)

♦ **He has a memorable product.** The very name "ShamWow" has a lot to do with its success. Consumers now connect Shlomi's name with the product itself, and people remember the combination. While many ads are memorable, consumers don't connect this memorability with the product name or its purpose. Shlomi has unmistakably linked the two—and it works.

♦ **He looks like he's having fun.** Too many people on TV look like they're doing a job, whereas Shlomi seems to be having a ball showing off the way his products work. In fact, in the Slap Chop ad, you almost get the impression that he's *winking* at you while the commercial is going on, as if to say, "Do you believe I get *paid* to do this?"

Interestingly enough, Shlomi *doesn't* get paid to endorse the products he represents—he owns the company that sells them. In the CNBC interview, Shlomi revealed that he has no desire to be in the infomercial business; in fact, he's really in the film business.

Vince Offer Shlomi was the writer, director, and star of a low-budget B-movie released in 1999 called *The Underground Comedy Movie*. Film critics called it one of the worst pieces of cinema ever created. Its own trailer stated that the film was "guaranteed to offend everybody," but, of course, that statement would only apply to those who chose to endure the film itself. The cast featured such notable names as Joey Buttafuoco, *The Green Mile*'s Michael Clarke Duncan, and Slash from the band *Guns 'n Roses*. Anna Nicole Smith was to have appeared in the movie as well, but backed out at the last minute—costing Shlomi $100,000. The film was a failure from a financial standpoint; that is, until Shlomi found himself watching late-night TV infomercials and decided that his film could be sold using the same methods. He created a commercial from the movie's trailer, ran it on the cable channel *Comedy Central*—and eventually sold 50,000 units that way.

Shlomi then decided that he wanted to branch out from the young male demographic and looked for a product to sell that would appeal to more mainstream consumers. He looked for a cleaning product that would be easy to demonstrate, and in 2006, he settled on a chamois cloth he found that was manufactured in Germany.

The first few names he wanted for the cloth didn't pass muster; "Sham It Up!" and "Shamit" were early rejects. "Then I realized that every time I demonstrated the product, people would say 'wow,'" said Shlomi in the CNBC interview. "So I thought of the name ShamWow, and the tagline, 'You'll say wow every time.'"

The rest, as they say, is now television history.

"BUT I'M NOT ON TV! HOW CAN I BE QUOTED?"

It's not necessary for 800-Pound Gorillas to be national or international presences to be quoted. They only need to define their market size, decide who they're going to be, and ruthlessly attack that segment by being meaningful to those they serve.

Steve Wallace is the owner of Wally's Wine and Spirits, an upscale liquor retailer in the Los Angeles area. The Zagat Survey has rated Wally's the number one wine store in all of L.A., with an incredible assortment of wines, spirits, and gift ideas.

In an interview with business marketing expert and author Lynda Resnick (http://blog.lyndaresnick.com/ cate gory/success-in-business/), Wallace reveals that Wally's has become an 800-Pound Gorilla—or a business that others follow. "Suppliers come to us," he says. "We're not Costco or Neiman Marcus, but they consider us [to be] a trend-setter, and we try to maintain that image."

Because his business is located near Hollywood, Wally's has become the go-to beverage store for many movie stars and celebrities in the area, and Wally's suppliers are very interested in that clientele. He uses that leverage extremely well. "[Suppliers] come to us and say, 'Pick 300 of your best customers. Send them up a bottle and tell them that you like the product.' You'd be surprised how many of these high-profile people send back a handwritten note. Then those suppliers go around to other retailers and say, 'Wally's is selling this product.'"

Wallace calls himself a "cowbell" for the suppliers with whom he works. "We set trends, so we've been able to leverage ourselves with these big companies with a lot of promotions. Since we're small, they pay for the product, and we send it out. The supplier will [work on these kinds of campaigns] with us, and the customers are happy."

Wally's also does a great deal of grassroots marketing. "I tell everybody to think small. We do a lot of small projects." For example, the upscale product review magazine *Robb Report* came to Wally's with an idea. "They wanted us to send to all our best customers a free subscription for a year to the *Robb Report*. We perfected a way to get the magazine to the people and a letter from us saying it was a free subscription for a year. That way, no one saw their addresses but me."

Wallace is always thinking creatively to capitalize on current trends. "I buy Google Adwords every day, but [recently] I bought 'Obama wines.' He had certain wines that he drank at the inauguration that I have in stock. So if you Google 'Obama wines' or 'inaugural wines,' it comes up with [a link to] Wally's Wine and Spirits."

Wally's proves that your universe doesn't have to be national or even regional to make an impact with your voice, your knowledge, and your expertise. When it comes to being quoted, if Wally's says it's good, you can take it to the bank—and that's a goal worthy of anyone in the sales profession who wants to be a dominant player.

WHAT'S YOUR QUOTE?

McDonald's has successfully branded a five-note advertising melody, followed by the often-quoted phrase, "I'm Lovin' It." John Madden of NFL broadcast fame made a career out of using the word, "boom!" to describe a big hit on the football field. Game show host Howie Mandel brought Americans the iconic question, "Deal or No

Deal?" The list of quotable 800-Pound Gorillas is nearly endless.

On a more local level, wherever you live and work, there are people you know that are quotable—from the corner coffee shop waitress and the package delivery guy to your regular customers and the company CEO.

So what's the quote that others would identify with you?

Consider how *your* words are recognized by those with whom you come into contact—and, more important, how you *want* to be recognized.

TAKEAWAYS

Being Quoted

♦ **Being an expert in your field at the 800-Pound Gorilla level means that others are listening and paying attention to what you have to say.** It means your opinions, thoughts, and actions are being watched and heeded by those who matter in your industry.

♦ **When you speak with a high degree of authority, people will listen, pay attention, and even quote you.** Experts are the ones who are quoted most often, and 800-Pound Gorillas demonstrate their expertise in the words they choose to use.

♦ **The dominant players in every field are watched, emulated, and quoted more often than anyone else.** Few people want to quote an average sales rep, support an average company, or write about an average product or service. But if you're an extraordinary thought leader in your chosen field, others will seek you out.

- **If you want to be quoted, being outrageous, different, or cutting-edge can work in your favor.** Controversy sells; and for some dominant players, it's the formula for their success. If you can find an angle to ethically exploit, it may be worth pursuing.
- **You don't have to have a national or international presence to find value in being quoted.** Just be sure you have something to say that's worthwhile, different, and easily attributable to you—and that your target market is listening.

SPEAK THE LANGUAGE OF YES, BUT TAKE NO FOR AN ANSWER

How 800-Pound Gorillas Get Beyond Rejection in Selling

Our family moved into a new home in November of 2008, and we put hardwood floors in a good portion of the main level. We've never had hardwood floors before, and for the first six months I've caught myself just walking around and admiring it. New hardwood flooring is just gorgeous to behold; no discolorations, no nicks or scratches, just a beautiful, natural finish all around.

We are a dog family, and before our move to this new house we lost Zena, our 10-year-old Rottweiler/Shepherd mix. Ever since we moved, my entire family has been on me to get a new puppy at this new house. What they don't understand is that my responsibility to our hardwood floors is to resist for as long as I can.

Dogs have toenails. Bigger dogs have bigger toenails; and our family has not been prone to choose the "toy" kinds of dogs. Throughout our 21-year marriage, my wife Sherri and I have had two Rottweilers and Zena, our Rott/Shepherd mix—and each one has weighed 110 pounds or more.

I still love dogs, too. I'm just not ready to initiate our beautiful wood floors yet.

I have rejected their pleas dozens of times already. Yet, they know that eventually, I will buckle under and say "Yes" to a new puppy, and I will love that little mutt just as much as they do.

If you've been in sales for any length of time, you've no doubt had eventual clients that initially said no. Many buyers believe that an initial rejection is one way of testing you as to what you're made of as a salesperson. If you survive the first seven or eight no's, they reason, then you really must believe in your product, and so maybe they should talk to you after all.

The number one thing that all successful 800-Pound Gorillas learn is this: Preparation for rejection is the best antidote for it.

CAN YOU TAKE IT?

How does a dominant salesperson prepare for rejection? In the following ways:

♦ Learn all the reasons that the prospect should buy.

♦ Prepare to answer all the reasons a prospect will give for not buying.
♦ Present with the confidence that a "yes" is the right answer for *both* parties.

Stephen Reynolds is Thailand's 800-Pound Gorilla of sales training, with major clients like GlaxoSmithKline, Philips Electronics, and Bangkok Hospital. Reynolds is based in the capitol city of Bangkok, but is originally from the suburbs of Chicago, Illinois, where he sold a number of products including insurance, credit card processing services, autos, and network marketing.

Reynolds admits that when he began his sales career, he was not the best. "I sold just enough of my products to not get fired," he says. Frustrated, he became a missionary and moved to Thailand in 1998, where he found a new life—including his wife. Soon afterward, with a new family and a baby on the way, he suddenly had a reason to be much better at what he did for a living.

"I took a job that I knew I couldn't do," Reynolds recalls. "I accepted a telemarketing sales position, selling call options on Euro currencies against the dollar as investment vehicles to customers in New Zealand and Australia from a boiler room in Bangkok." He was impressed by the company's ability to sell *him* on the benefits of its product. "I learned a great deal about how to sell from listening to my trainers in the class," he says. "I was way out of my comfort zone, but I had bills to pay, and I did see the value of the product, so I was determined to succeed."

Not satisfied with the limited education he was receiving from the company, Reynolds went out and bought 12 different books on sales and read all of them in six weeks. The collection included classics like Roger Dawson's *Secrets of Power Negotiating, SPIN Selling* by Neil Rackham, and *The Closers* by Ben Gay III, as well as *Secrets of Question-Based Selling* by Robert Freese, *The Power to Get In* by Michael Boylan, and *The Art of the Hard Sell* by Robert Shook. Reynolds was energized by those books, and in three months he became one of the top 3 percent of all the salespeople in the company.

"I had to get beyond that first rejection before I really started to kick it into high gear," Reynolds explains. "It was because of all the studying I did on answering objections—and how not to give up on each call—that I was able to succeed."

Reynolds distinctly remembers reading and memorizing a "last-chance objection handler" line from one of his 12 sales books. "It was for the prospect that gives you multiple reasons for not buying, and the suggested comeback for that from the book was, 'I understand what you're saying, but that wouldn't stop you from buying today, would it?' I memorized it—even though it sounded so corny to me at the time."

Sure enough, just three days later, Reynolds was engaged in conversation with a prospect. "Stephen, there are five reasons why I'm not buying today," said the prospect. "Number one, I only have $3,000; number two, my wife would kill me; number three, I would never send money to Bangkok from Australia for any reason; number four, I don't know you at all; and number five, I think the investment is far too risky."

It was like interacting in slow motion, Reynolds recalls. "I paused for a moment, and then I heard myself say, 'Well, sir, I understand what you're saying, but that wouldn't stop you from buying today, would it?' My brain was on autopilot. I had nothing to lose, so I just thought—why not?"

There was silence on the other end for nearly 20 seconds.

"No, that wouldn't stop me from buying," the prospect said calmly.

"My jaw dropped," Reynolds says. "It was at that moment that I really understood the logic of selling. I was overthinking it. Rejection was only a temporary 'no' to what someone may very well want to say 'yes' to, and I just needed to find the right combination of truthful words—not lies or deception—to unlock that."

Reynolds uses that story today to energize and inspire the sales reps he trains.

IT'S ONLY "NO" FOR TODAY

All 800-Pound Gorillas understand that everyone has a certain number of no's in them, and some have more than others. The key is determining how many no's a person will put out there before that individual finally sees what you see—and says yes.

Louis Lautman understands the words "yes" and "no" extremely well. As you may recall from Chapter 1, Lautman is the executive producer of *The YES Movie*, the inspirational film about young millionaires and how they achieved success.

When he began the movie project, Lautman faced plenty of rejection from individuals, companies, and organizations that were concerned about the fact that he had no film industry experience—and that didn't share his vision of the finished product. Lautman's background in selling, however, had prepared him well. "I've been selling things out of my little red wagon since I was four years old," he says. "I sold pretzels to my neighbors, baseball cards, electronics, and hair replacement systems. You name it, I've sold it."

Lautman's ability to take rejection in stride is due in large part to a door-to-door sales job he took in New York in the late 1990s. "I was selling people on the chance to save money on their phone bills and get high-speed Internet access. My boss told me, 'Lou, get out there and knock on 50 doors a day.' So I knocked on those 50 doors, and on each occasion I made a decision. If I made a presentation and I didn't sell them, I developed this mind-set of 'okay,' I sat with them, I informed them, and they didn't say yes today. That wasn't a no forever. It was just a matter of no until something changes—until I get more creative, until their existing provider does them wrong, or something else. The door is never closed."

That mind-set would serve him well in *The Yes Movie* project.

Lautman asked dozens of successful millionaires and thought leaders if they'd like to be interviewed for potential inclusion in the film. Many said yes—including well-known motivational voices like T. Harv Eker, Bob Proctor, and Mark Victor Hansen; other lesser-known but equally successful entrepreneurs like Ben Casnocha of Comcate.com, Katrina Campins of *The Apprentice*, and Dan "Punkass" Caldwell of TapOut Clothing also signed on.

There was one individual in particular, however, that Lautman badly wanted to include in the movie—but he turned it down.

"I really wanted Richard Branson in *The Yes Movie*," he says. "Most people told me that I was crazy to even ask him. 'Richard Branson? What the heck? How could you even think of doing something like that?' But when I hear something like that, I'm the one that says, 'Why *not* me?'"

Even though Sir Richard turned him down for this project, Lautman's rejection philosophy was in full gear. "I got a no from Richard for now, but the door is still open, and that doesn't mean I can't partner with him on some other project in the future."

And knowing Louis, I have no doubt that he and Sir Richard will be working on something very soon.

WANT TO BE AN AUTHOR? GET READY FOR REJECTION

Ask any aspiring author about what it takes to become published, and no doubt you'll receive a myriad of answers. "Publishers are ruthless!" some will say. "They send you letters that say they've reviewed your manuscript and that it 'doesn't fit what they're looking for right now,' and they've never even read what you sent! They have hundreds of unsolicited manuscripts that they pile in this giant closet of a room, with the packages unopened. It's called the 'slush pile,' and they put people they don't like in there and tell them to search through the rubble for something that might sell."

Or you might hear how others have been rejected dozens of times from traditional publishers, as they vow never to buy one of their authors' books again.

I never went through any of that. Most authors are not salespeople, which makes them highly susceptible to Rejection Disease. I just decided that I wasn't going to be rejected, but that someone simply needed to see the wisdom that I obviously was going to bring to some lucky publisher's life.

Book Expo America is the annual trade show for the book industry that features rows and rows of publishers,

authors, and suppliers—all of whom are eager to talk about
the industry and give out books. My first Book Expo was
at McCormick Place in Chicago, just an hour's drive from
my home, and I talked to authors, publishers, and anyone
else who would listen to my questions.

The next year, I decided that I needed to talk to more
authors to find out how they became published. Since I
worked for a radio station, I wore my station's logo polo
shirt, borrowed the cassette tape recorder from the station's news department, and pretended to be on a reporting
mission.

I had carefully scripted my approach to each author:
*"Hi, I'm from a suburban Chicago radio station, and I'm interviewing
authors for a potential radio segment. Would you mind answering a
few questions?"*

Hungry for publicity of any kind for their new books,
the authors were only too happy to oblige. I asked five
questions, all written down on a legal pad:

1. What is the title of your book, and what is it about?
2. Who does your book appeal to?
3. How long did it take you to write it?
4. What was the most difficult part about the process
   of writing it?
5. What would be your single best piece of advice to
   an agent-less, unpublished author in today's marketplace?

I heard fascinating stories from dozens of people—
from teenagers to seniors, PhD's to unschooled
individuals—from all walks of life. Each was very
generous in describing to me their various heartaches,
trials, and challenges in birthing their books. A few had no

challenges at all; the publishers had actually approached them to write their books. Others had used thousands of dollars of their own money to self-publish, in the hopes that a major publisher would see their book, like it, and buy the rights. The stories were as different as snowflakes, but their number one piece of advice was nearly universal: *Don't give up.*

That was it.

Many of them had been turned down by other publishers, struggled with lack of support from family or friends, had personal tragedy interrupt their journey, and had experienced a hundred other things that stood in their way. Several told stories of their many rejections from certain publishers and how they kept trying with others until they finally got a yes from someone.

Those who were the most successful didn't allow rejection to determine whether their books were good enough to be thrust upon the world. They took rejection in stride, made the necessary changes, whether it was in their style, their manuscript, or their approach, and never, ever gave up.

It may seem very simple, but for those who dominate in sales today, it is the ultimate secret of success.

TAKEAWAYS

Getting Beyond Rejection in Sales

- **Rejection is not personal; it's a lesson in how to become more dominant.** Without knowing why people say no to you, it's impossible to improve on your product or your presentation.
- **The very best in sales are rejected more often than you might think.** No one ever sees the countless

rejections that today's dominant companies or reps faced on their way to becoming dominant players.

♦ **Getting prepared for rejection will help you fight through it.** Learn all the reasons someone should say yes to you; then learn all the comebacks to the reasons they won't buy. Your presentation should then be given with the confidence that if your product is a good fit, rejection is not an option.

♦ **A no is just no for today.** All 800-Pound Gorillas understand the time value of relationships and that some of tomorrow's customers are ones that had to say no yesterday before they could say yes.

♦ **Don't give up.** Don't give up. Don't give up.

10

WHERE THE LEOPARDS HANG OUT

Why 800-Pound Gorillas Know Their Competition

Gorillas have very few natural predators to worry about. Humans are by far their number one threat, but because of their size, strength, and intelligence, most other animals just don't have the guts to stand up to that formidable of a beast.

In fact, the only known natural predator of gorillas is the leopard. There have been records of leopards attacking smaller or sicker gorillas, and so gorillas have been known to look for clues as to the whereabouts of nearby leopards and to stay clear.

If you know more about those who are against you, it's easier to survive.

That premise is true in many areas of life—including college basketball. With broadcast TV rights, alumni donations, the university's positive national reputation, and so much more riding on each season—there has never been more pressure on college athletic programs to succeed. The more you know about an opposing team, the better you can put a game plan together.

When the NCAA Division I Basketball Tournament brackets are announced in March, many teams that have never seen each other play during the course of their regular season end up being paired against each other. Game films, or video of the opposing team's past performances, are typically what a coaching staff will use to get the knowledge they need; but it's not easy to get film of teams that you don't know very well, or worse, those that don't play televised games often.

Enter Hoop 1 Video.

For just $30 per game (or $60 during the "hot season" or the NCAA tournament), you can get nearly any video of any mens' college basketball game that was played anywhere in the country. Missed that big game between Xavier and Miami of Ohio back in November? No problem; Hoop 1's got the whole thing for 30 bucks (www.hoop1.com). By watching the films, coaches can get an idea of what kind of game plan to use to prepare their players. Without the films, they would have to depend on hearsay, notes from others, and trial and error—which would make for a very uneasy game on both sides.

Sounds a little bit like some of the unprepared sales calls that are made every day—hearsay, scribbled notes, and trial and error.

KEEP YOUR FRIENDS CLOSE ... AND YOUR COMPETITIVE DATA CLOSER

U.K. sales training company executive Sean McPheat—whom we met in Chapter 2—calls his preproposal competitive analysis his single biggest advantage in selling his company's services to others.

"Every quarter, our staff updates the data files on each of our sales training competitors in the marketplace," McPheat says. He won't go into great detail on each item he studies for proprietary reasons, but suffice it to say that their research is, in his words, "exhaustive by anyone's measure."

One specific item that McPheat updates is how the competition is portraying his company, MTD Sales Training, to others. "I want to know specifically what they have to say about us and our systems, so that when I enter a meeting, I know what the competition may have already told the prospect about me, and I can adjust my presentation to counter those things which may have been related about us to them."

If they know who they're bidding against—which they *do* know about 80 percent of the time—McPheat's people use that as an advantage. "We know the competitions' products, their probable solutions, what those products cost, their presentation styles, the quality of their proposals—even who from their companies was likely to have given their presentations. With that kind of knowledge, we can position our product in line with our competitors, and we feel very confident that we can win most every time."

How is he doing? McPheat's current closing ratio is about 70 percent—which certainly justifies all that effort to know his competition.

AN INSIDE JOB

Sean McPheat gains his competitive advantage by researching the competition to become an insider. Of course, nothing gets you closer to the competition than actually having been a former customer of the products yourself.

Brian Silengo is a hotelier by trade who now works in a company that serves the hotel industry. As associate vice president for TIG Global—a supplier of interactive web marketing tools for the hospitality industry—Silengo leads a team that sells the most expensive—and, arguably, the most valuable—set of online services for premier hotels and destinations around the world.

"Eighty-five percent of travelers now go to the Web to book travel," says Silengo. "Those in the travel business have to maximize their exposure to this group, and that's what our company helps them to do." Through a combination of Web design, booking engines, web site optimization, and pay-per-click search systems, TIG Global has grown from a $20 million firm to over $50 million in just two short years under Silengo's sales leadership.

One of the keys to Silengo's success is his background in the industry. As a fast-track executive with Marriott Hotels for six years, he learned the industry and the needs of the properties from the inside. That knowledge has allowed him to excel at TIG Global. "Our approach to the online sales business—our DNA—comes from the hotelier side. We're not simply a technology company that just happens to service the hospitality industry. Two of our owners are former Marriott presidents, so we thoroughly understand what the properties are all about, what they need, and what they don't need."

Coming from the hotel industry, Silengo was familiar with all the vendors of his kind of product. When he first began at TIG Global, however, the same few competitors came up consistently in bidding situations, so he set out to study each of them to learn how to sell against them. "Knowing as many people in the industry as I did, I asked for their help in gathering the info I needed on the competition and broke it down—not just at the brochure level, but with actual user data, talking to people who have used each of the competing systems to learn their pros and cons." He knew, for example, that service levels were a big issue for his customers. "In hospitality, service is everything. If something goes down, there has to be an immediate response and an immediate fix. We're highly responsive, and have dedicated people to deliver that kind of service. It costs more per month for our service, but our fee includes an unlimited number of service calls, with a dedicated service staff. I know from my research that our competition has a lower cost per month, but charges a lot of money for each service call—which can push the monthly bill far higher than ours."

It's that sort of comparative information that gives Silengo an advantage in negotiations. "When any of our people are on a sales call and a competitor's product is mentioned, we can immediately compare and contrast our features with theirs—both the good and the bad. Because we know all the features of everyone's products, we can help the customer make the right decision based on a true apples-to-apples comparison."

KNOWLEDGE IS POWER(FUL)

Is it important to know your competition as well as Sean McPheat and Brian Silengo?

Only if you want to provide clear, compelling selling statements that you can control during the sales
process.

Craig Cerretani knows this very well. We met Craig in
Chapter 4 as one of the founders of Longfellow Benefits, an
employee benefits firm in the Boston area that specializes
in programs for companies with 75 to 1,500 workers.

"We have plenty of competition, but many of our key
people have worked for them at one time or another, and
[so] we understand how they operate," says Cerretani. "The
larger players in our field have a great sales staff—an 'A-
Team' that comes in to do their presentations. These guys
are very competent, extremely capable. Because of their
size, however, once they've sold that account, they hand
things off to people the client will never see. Now, is that
a bad thing or a good thing? It all depends on how you
present it."

On the other hand, many of Cerretani's presentations
are made with several of his key people in the room at the
same time. He explains that they're not simply representatives of the company; they're the actual people who will
be working on the clients' behalf.

"[During] a presentation I'll say, 'Mr. Prospect, I'm glad
that you and your team are assembled here. That's good;
you want people around you that will be involved in this
decision on a day-to-day basis. We do too, and that's why
I've brought my team here today.' I then go on to explain,
'When you see our competition, ask them who's actually doing the work *behind* those blue suits. They're very
good, but they're also very *big*. You won't meet and get
to know the people who are actually doing the work and
making things happen for you. Let me introduce you to
my staff—the people who *will* get to know you *personally*;
who *you* will get to know *yourself*; and who will be actively

involved in managing your business with us.' And then I
go around the table and introduce my senior vice presidents and managing directors of each of our company's
departments.

"It's a powerful differentiator; and it's been very successful for us when we're competing with bigger, less personal
firms."

BE VISIBLE

Research is important; but you can always take knowing
your competition one step further. What if you were the
"visible expert" on your subject; the person to whom others
naturally came with information?

Gary Dale Cearley is president of Global Projects
Logistics Network—one of the largest and fastest-
growing business-to-business freight logistics networks
in the world. GPLN's members specialize in project
cargo—which includes dozens of shipping companies in
over 150 countries and which gives cargo owners access
to a large number of experts in getting things from Point
A to Point B.

Cearley has come to be known as an expert because
of his visibility in the industry, and because he's visible,
he gets to see and hear things about the competition that
no one else does. He attends several annual industry exhi-
bitions around the world promoting the company and its
network—in places like Antwerp, Munich, Shanghai, and
Moscow. He also puts on his own international conferences
four times a year, so that his network can meet and grow
and learn from each other. With 20 years' experience in
the international logistics industry, he's frequently invited
to speaking engagements as an expert, and is often quoted
in industry news sources.

"'I actually do very little of what you would call pure sales work," says Cearley. "When I present our network to a potential member, all of the hard work is done beforehand."

The "hard work," as Cearley calls it, is all the research, prequalifying, and preparation to find the clients that are right for GPLN. "It's much easier to sell a company that you know is a perfect fit for your product than to do cold-calling or prospecting." A perfect prospect for Cearley is a company that's independently owned, has a solid reputation in its home market, and has several years' experience doing project cargo. "We won't take on anyone in the network that doesn't fit," says Cearley. "There's too much at stake for everybody involved. Each member in the network is a reflection on everyone else, and so my role is to protect the reputation of the group as the best of the best at what they do."

Because of the way that he prequalifies clients, Cearley's competition is nearly nonexistent—even though GPLN's annual dues are 50 percent higher than others in the industry. "Our competitor is bigger than we are, but we're growing many times faster even though we're priced higher. I know the weaknesses of my competition, so I only choose to pursue the companies that are a perfect fit for us. We're already considered the most effective network, and it won't be long before we'll be the biggest in size."

If knowledge is power, then competitive data is the stuff that 800-Pound Gorillas are made of.

TAKEAWAYS

Know Your Competition

♦ **800-Pound Gorillas get to know all they can about the competition.** Whether they have experience in their camp, knowledge through friends or contacts, research on their own, or training from their own company—the dominant players know the others' strengths and weaknesses and can discuss them proficiently with their prospects.

♦ **Customers want to deal with suppliers who are well-rounded, knowledgeable, and understand all the available options in their industry.** They may not always want their opinion, but often customers do want to know that sales reps can be called on to discuss options—both theirs and the competition's—in a knowledgeable way.

♦ **It helps to have a background that will facilitate getting to know more about your competition.** Whether you've worked for a vendor, a buyer, or a competitor, using your knowledge and contacts can be very valuable in winning more business, grabbing market share, and becoming a more dominant player.

♦ **Being visible can help in the collection of competitive data.** Writing articles, starting discussion groups, attending trade shows, and speaking at conferences can put you in a more dominant position and even help you acquire competitive data, if used properly.

11

IT'S MORE FUN TO BEAT YOUR CHEST AND ROAR

Why 800-Pound Gorillas Bring Passion to All They Do

If you're dumb enough not to know that something can't be done, you'll go ahead and try it anyway. And sometimes, you'll actually succeed.

When I landed my first job in sales, most people at the company didn't give me a snowball's chance in a fireplace to succeed. WBYG-FM was a 50,000-watt blowtorch of a radio station 30 miles south of Chicago. The station's general manager, Howard Dybedock, was a generous man who genuinely seemed to like me. He knew that I had worked diligently as a part-time on-air DJ for several years, and he knew I really wanted to be a full-time disc jockey, but there were no positions open at the time I graduated from college in May of 1983.

"We'd like to hire you, Bill," Howard said as he sat across his desk from me at my post-college job interview. "Trouble is, the only position we have available is a new sales position we're thinking about creating. We think there's money to be had in our northern listening area, but we've never had anyone go up there full-time to sell advertising. Are you interested?" He offered me $125 a week and some weekend hours on the air if I wanted them.

I had nothing to lose. I was young, I was living at home, I had few expenses, and this was the place I had always wanted to work full-time someday. I took the job, thinking it would be a short-term gig until an on-air position opened up.

Little did I know that no one else had taken the job because none of them thought it could be a viable way to make a living. I didn't know that the territory had never been sold before, and that it was a tough place to sell advertising. I didn't know that since we weren't a "Chicago station," we weren't considered important to the big advertisers. I didn't know that no one in the south Chicago suburbs had even heard of WBYG much less had interest in advertising with us.

Good thing nobody filled me in before I started.

I fearlessly drove the 30 miles north each day to towns like South Chicago Heights, Homewood, Matteson, Flossmoor, and Crete. I knocked on the door of anyone who looked like they had customers that listened to rock-and-roll radio. I asked lots of questions, told our story with excitement and enthusiasm, and wrote an order or two every now and then.

A month went by. Then two. At the end of three months, I had sold a decent amount of advertising, but despite great guidance from my sales manager, Kathy Gagliano, I still didn't feel like I was getting the hang of it.

Then I found Seaway Honda.

Seaway Honda was a small motorcycle and ATV dealership in Chicago Heights, owned by a local husband-and-wife team. Its showroom held maybe 10 bikes tops, and business was okay but not booming. They were just selling enough to get by, and they seemed comfortable with that.

I saw their place as I was canvassing the area one day and was excited about the possibilities as I pulled into the small parking lot. Rock-n-roll and motorcycles! This was going to be *big*! I thought to myself.

The pair who ran Seaway were the nicest people I had met since I had been on the job. They filled me in on what the business had done, how they'd advertised in the past, and how they wanted to grow their customer base beyond the immediate area, especially to the south near Kankakee, which is where my station broadcast from. They weren't familiar with WBYG, but they flipped it on in the showroom while we were meeting and liked what they heard. Because they saw my passion for the station, and they had some Honda co-op advertising money from the manufacturer that they hadn't used—and saw no better way to use it—they asked if I would help them spend it properly on my station.

"Absolutely!" I responded excitedly. "Let's put your money to work for you!"

Up to that point, the other full-time employees at the station looked at me as the running joke. I was always happy to be there, full of enthusiasm and smiles and compliments, and apparently, I drove a few of them crazy. They created a nickname for me that they kept a secret for years: I was "Eddie," which was short for the brown-nosing-yet-mischievous Eddie Haskell from *Leave It to Beaver*.

When "Eddie" brought the sizable order from Seaway Honda into the station, they stopped laughing. "That was a lucky sale," they said. "Anyone can get an order like that once. Let's see if he can get a reorder."

When I brought in the second Seaway Honda order—a much larger one—they all took notice.

By Christmas of that year, I had hit my stride. I had billed a sizable percentage of the total advertising for the station for December, and it was then that I realized that I was doing something that hadn't been done before, albeit in an unconventional way. I was becoming an 800-Pound Gorilla.

PASSION: A VALUABLE COMMODITY

As a young sales rep fresh out of college, I had no business succeeding to the degree that I had. The one thing I had going for me was passion: passion for the station, for the music format, for my clients, for creativity in advertising, and for life.

David Siteman Garland shares that same passion.

Garland is a bold, energetic entrepreneur and president of The David Siteman Garland Agency—a busy marketing and PR firm in St. Louis, Missouri. He is the creator and host of his own half-hour business TV program, *The Rise to the Top*, which airs on the ABC television network affiliate in St. Louis (www.TheRiseToTheTop.com), a venture that he started by breaking the mold on how sponsorships are created and sold.

Oh, and by the way—Garland is just 24 years old.

"I truly believe that in life you're either remarkable or ordinary," he says. "I've always wanted to be remarkable in every way possible. When you're ordinary, you blend in, and there's no success in that. When you challenge what's ordinary, great things happen."

This fear of "the way it's always been done" began early in Garland's life. At Washington University in St. Louis, Garland was afraid of taking an ordinary major. "Everybody else had these boring majors, and I wanted something that was different and that interested me—so I majored in Women's Studies." He claims to be the only straight white male to have earned a degree in Women's Studies from Washington University. (The University confirmed Garland's degree but could not officially confirm the rest.)

When Garland graduated, he was crazy for inline hockey, a game played on a hard surface using inline roller skates instead of ice skates. "There were plenty of inline teams playing, but there wasn't any kind of organized league, so I created one"—from scratch. Garland began the PIHA, or Professional Inline Hockey Association, with six teams—four from the St. Louis area, one from Chicago, and one from Cincinnati. Their first game was played in October 2006—barely five months after Garland had graduated from college.

The trouble was that the only person who initially seemed excited about sponsoring the PIHA was Garland himself. "I literally got kicked out of each place I went to," he recalls. "I went in spewing out all the information I had about the PIHA, and people didn't want to hear it. I eventually figured it out. I started each meeting by asking, 'What would be your *ideal* sponsorship opportunity?' I learned that

I had to listen instead of speak. I found out what they were looking for, and then I went and created it."

Garland's first sponsor was Shell Oil Company, which was willing to take a risk on his enthusiasm. Other corporate giants soon followed—including Anheuser-Busch, Pepsi, and Mobil Oil. With that experience under his belt, The David Siteman Garland Agency now creates innovative sponsorships for a wide range of clients (www.dsgagency.com).

On Garland's TV program, sponsors get much more than just a commercial spot. "I've trashed the concept of the 30-second commercial," says Garland. "People get to create their own value-added portions of the program. For example, our attorney sponsor gets a chance to talk about a law-related Q&A as a part of the show. Our interview segments are branded just like many of the sports broadcasts you see. We're not afraid of trying something new and seeing what happens."

In keeping with Garland's style, *The Rise to the Top* has fear-of-ordinary written all over it. "This is *not* your grandfather's business show!" Garland proudly proclaims in the introduction, showing a white-haired gentleman with a red slash through his photo. "If you're wearing pleated pants, this show is *not* for you!" he says moments later, as a pair of pleated pants comes up on the screen with its own red circle and slash.

Garland's passion for his clients, his viewers, and his cause appears to be working; the first seven episodes in 2009 had a combined TV viewership of a half-million people. Sponsors are lining up to be a part of the program, and Garland sees a potential syndication or licensing deal in the works. "Licensing a TV concept has never been done before," he says proudly, "which is why I'll probably end up doing it."

A PASSION FOR SUCCESS

Successful people just naturally want to hang out with guys like David Siteman Garland. He's a great example of the positive things that can happen when you breathe passion into your work.

A lot of that same passion can be felt in the world of professional sports—but in places that may surprise you.

While it may seem looking in from the outside that the world of professional sports is all glamorous, just as in many other industries, there are elements on the inside that most people never see. One of those is the sports ticket sales department.

The majority of professional sports teams don't have waiting lists of fans begging to buy their tickets. Even though they receive tens of millions of dollars in publicity value in the media, there are still thousands of tickets that need to be proactively sold in order to fill the stands game after game. And that's where the sales department comes in.

Many teams hire a legion of account reps who place dozens of sales phone calls a day to businesses, individuals, and groups, selling various ticket opportunities ranging from full-season luxury box programs to economical mini-plans of several games each. It's a tough, grind-'em-out kind of job, but for the right individual it's an exciting and rewarding occupation with lots of high-profile potential and energy.

Chris Terwoord was the top season ticket sales rep in the entire National Hockey League in the 2007-08 season.

Terwoord sold a record $3.4 million in season tickets for the Chicago Blackhawks—a team that experienced a rebirth in popularity in Chicago during his record-breaking selling season. But even during a good year and with a championship team (which the Blackhawks were *not*)—$3.4 million in sales is an insane amount for a single rep to bring in. Most reps in professional sports don't sell a fraction of that amount. So how did Terwoord do it?

While several things happened simultaneously to bring Chris the success he experienced, the most important thing that he did was *not* to fear the bad reputation of the team. When Chris arrived in Chicago in the summer of 2006, the Blackhawks were in fan disarray, an afterthought in Chicago sports. They hadn't made the playoffs in several years, and team owner Bill Wirtz was unpopular with the fans because of his legendary eccentric actions. He didn't televise Blackhawks games because he felt the privilege of watching the Hawks should be reserved for those who put their hard-earned money down to see them live. He was reputed to treat players badly, squeeze the budgets tightly (earning the nickname "Dollar Bill"), and shut out several former star players like Bobby Hull, Tony Esposito, and Stan Mikita. He even fired popular play-by-play announcer Pat Foley in favor of someone else.

"I had no idea of the management and ownership issues when I came to town," says Terwoord. "I was just excited to be in Chicago and selling for a legendary franchise. I wasn't as negative as everyone else who had been in town for a while. All I had experienced was the success I had in my previous position in ticket sales with the Cleveland Cavaliers, and I was anxious to bring those skills to Chicago."

Terwoord has a passion for success.

With the Cavaliers, Terwoord was trained to make 125 individual calls per day, which he did successfully. "That's all I knew how to do, and so I decided that good reputation or not, I was going to establish myself as *the* guy to go to for Chicago Blackhawks tickets. If things were going to turn around for the team, then all the people I was talking to would know exactly who to see."

So—armed with a telephone and a list of prospects—Terwoord started to work. "I talked to everyone. I didn't care who they were, who they worked for. I was just going to work my butt off. Even if they said no, I got their mailing address or their e-mail address and sent them something—a business card, an e-mail, whatever. I was planting seeds everywhere."

Terwoord says he was much more patient with people on the phones than some of his peers. "I just let them talk. People were pretty frustrated about the team, and so I listened to their beefs, let them know I heard them, and tried to establish a relationship between them and the team. They just didn't feel like anyone from the team had been listening to them before, and that's what I could do to help."

Before long, Terwoord had a boatload of teed-up prospects, ready to buy if anything should change. And change it did.

In September of 2007, Bill Wirtz passed away after a brief battle with cancer. His son, Rocky Wirtz, took over as president, and his philosophy of spend-money-to-make-money was a stark contrast to his father's tightfistedness. Three weeks after his father's funeral, Rocky announced that he was in negotiations with Comcast SportsNet to broadcast a small number of Blackhawks games in Chicago for the first time in a generation. Six games were broadcast that year to great fanfare, and that led to broadcasts of the entire 82-game season the following year.

Rocky then hired John McDonough from the Chicago Cubs to be the team's new president; and McDonough worked to institute even more positive changes to the team. He reestablished relations with the Blackhawks greats of the past, brought back fan favorite Pat Foley to the broadcast booth, and made many other fan-friendly changes.

The team had the number one draft pick in the 2007 draft, and selected a young 18-year-old named Patrick Kane—an electrifying speedster on the ice. The Blackhawks had drafted another young standout named Jonathan Toews in 2006. Toews had been in the Hawks' farm system during the previous year, and they brought him up to partner with Kane. McDonough then opened up the team purse strings—once clenched so tightly—and signed Brian Campbell, an all-star free agent defenseman.

The timing was just right for someone who had planted lots of seeds in the marketplace for ticket sales.

"I could not have planned it any better," Terwoord recalls. "It was crazy. People were calling me left and right. Everything I had hoped would happen was all coming together."

Season tickets vary in price considerably, depending on the location of the seats. But Terwoord wasn't fond of selling anything but the seats close to the ice. "I had been to a lot of games, and I knew what the view was like in the 300 section. I wouldn't want to sit upstairs, so I sold seats in the places I knew I'd want to sit myself."

Terwoord's passion about seat locations came through on the phones. "My customers could tell that I was in love with the seats I was selling them. They could tell it in my voice. I would say, 'Look, you won't have the chance to get these seats again for a long time, and this is your chance. You're going to thank me later!' And they did."

According to Terwoord, a typical two-seat season ticket sale in the better sections of the United Center—for a full, 43-game home season—averaged between $7,000 and $11,000. "When I was getting close to the million-dollar mark in sales, I told myself, 'Wouldn't it be great? Let's go for that.' When I got there, I thought, 'What the hey? I'll go for one-point-five!' Then I got to two million, and I said, 'Wow! I'm here; why not go for three?' I hit three, and wanted to hit three and a half, but I was just short."

With the price level of the seats he was selling, Terwoord was able to get to his record-breaking total much sooner. "If I had been only selling the 300 section [the lower-priced seats], I would never have cracked a million," he recalls. "I just kept selling the good stuff until it was gone."

The Blackhawks' full season equivalent seats—or FSEs as they're called in the business—stood at under 4,000 seats in 2006-07. Over the next several months, with the help of Terwoord and the rest of the Blackhawks' sales staff, that number jumped to 14,000 season tickets sold (which they had to cut off because of other commitments), with a current waiting list of more than 5,000 fans.

"If I had let everyone else's attitude about the team rub off on me, I would never have experienced the success I have," Terwoord says.

The bottom line was that Chris Terwoord didn't let others' negative perception of the team become his reality. His passion for the positive aspects of the team, for his customers, and for his own success transcended everything else around him.

That's the kind of stuff 800-Pound Gorillas are made of.

TAKEAWAYS

Demonstrating Passion

♦ **Those companies and individuals who dominate their market bring a passion to their work that sets them apart from others.** You can sense it in the way they address others about their product, how they approach their job, and how they serve others. Those who are truly sold on their products and the things they can do to enhance others' lives are more passionate about what they do, and ultimately more successful.

♦ **Passionate people are way more fun to be around.** They're more confident, happier, and just seem to enjoy others' company more. Oh, and by the way—they're typically the leaders in their field.

♦ **Given a choice, prospects would generally prefer to do business with people who are passionate about their work.** It may be psychological, but most people tend to gravitate toward those who make them feel better about themselves. Passionate people like 800-Pound Gorillas have the knack of doing that far better than most others.

12

FORAGING, SHELTER, AND MATING

Why 800-Pound Gorillas Master the Fundamentals

Gorillas in the wild have few priorities. Besides eating, finding shelter, and socializing, there aren't many things that they consider to be necessary. As a gorilla, if you're not all that good at finding food, protecting yourself, or getting along with others, you may still survive, but you may not develop as well as some of the others.

For an 800-Pound Gorilla of sales, there are certain fundamentals in the business world as well. Many people survive without them, but for those who truly excel, there is a clear understanding of the value of these skills and activities to develop into a position of dominance in their field.

WHAT DO I HAVE TO KNOW?

Many companies set aside a certain number of hours each year for ongoing training of their people in several different skill sets. *Training* magazine's annual survey of the top 125 U.S. companies who administered company-sponsored training and development placed the world's largest professional services firm, PricewaterhouseCoopers, at the number one position in 2009—for the second year in a row. PwC's unbelievable menu of training includes traditional and virtual classroom courses, self-studies, team-based learning activities, action learning projects, coaching/mentoring frameworks, and large-scale conferences. The firm serves more than 150,000 discrete users each year with nearly 7,000 individual courses, more than 12,000 classroom-based sessions, and 19,701 web sessions. A large majority of those learning sessions are not for newbies but experienced pros who are looking to improve their basic skill sets.

(To learn more, visit www.nxtbook.com/nxtbooks/nielsen/training0209/index.php?startid=71#/30.)

Most companies don't do a fraction of what PwC does. However, whether it's sponsored by your company or you're taking the initiative on your own, there is a fundamental concept about learning: The one who's ultimately—and permanently—benefiting from any sort of training investment is *you*. If you're sitting around waiting for your company to train you, you're wasting valuable time that you could be spending taking control of your own career.

When I'm called in to help improve a company's skills (www. The800PoundGorilla.com), I'm typically met with one of several different kinds of scenarios. Sometimes the room is full of brand-new recruits, fresh out of college and eager to start, with very little—if any—prior sales training. Other times, I'm working with a blend of new hires and veterans who've been selling for years and have had multiple training sessions.

One particular NBA team with whom I've worked for a number of years has a core of veteran salespeople who have been through my training several times. I mix up the training message so that it's fresh for them, but much of what we go over is identical year after year. I'm always surprised and delighted when the three days of training are over, because most every member of the experienced crew will make it over to me at some point and tell me that they were so glad they were there because of some tidbit they picked up about the fundamentals. "It's so good for us to step back each year and work with Bill on the little things that make us successful," wrote one participant on his program evaluation.

It's not surprising that their sales team is consistently among the top performers in average annual per-game attendance in the entire NBA.

WHAT SHOULD I WORK ON?

In my sales training program, there are six fundamentals we work on consistently:

1. **A thorough knowledge of the product**, including how others use the product for their benefit or the benefit of others.
2. **A straightforward, confident opening** that states your purpose without trickery or false statements.

3. **A good, solid command of the right questions to ask** that uncover customer needs and help both seller and prospect to come to a mutually beneficial conclusion.

4. **An understanding of the most common objections**, what those objections might really mean, and a confident set of answers that clarify and move the prospect into a mutual understanding of the benefits.

5. **An ability to ask for the business** with the confidence and knowledge that everybody wins if the prospect says yes.

6. **The continual delivery of value for that customer over the long term**, creating perpetual confidence in the product and the provider.

There are of course other elements of sales success that top reps pursue, many of which we've talked about here; but these six are the ones that all 800-Pound Gorillas work on relentlessly. If these components of selling—discussed below in further detail—are rock-solid, the others seem to come much more naturally.

A Thorough Knowledge of the Product

The basics of the product or service's features are important to know, but even more important to the professional rep is having the ability to communicate the benefits it provides to those who use it. For example, in sports ticket sales, the product may be the physical seat at the ball game, the ticket itself, or the game on the field. But that's not what the prospect is truly *buying*. It's the value of that seat—the benefits it provides to the end user—that needs to be thoroughly understood, communicated, and sold to the prospect.

What value could a buyer of baseball tickets receive? Perhaps its spending more quality time with the family; entertaining key business clients; rewarding a top employee for a project well done; giving to a local charity for an auction; thanking someone special; wooing a future client away from the competition; or any number of positive outcomes. Sales pros sell value—benefits and outcomes—versus features; and the only way to do that is to know your product inside and out.

A Straightforward, Confident Opening

If you've ever heard a bad conversation opener from a sales rep, you know what to avoid: rambling, incompetent, slick, pandering, over-complimentary, syrupy, know-it-all, and whiney voices—methods that are all but ignored by today's prospects. I believe that most buyers know whether they're going to buy from a salesperson within the first several seconds of their first encounter.

First impressions have to be carefully considered, rehearsed, and updated frequently to avoid burnout and sing-song delivery. So many salespeople rely on whatever comes out of their head at the moment of a first impression with a potential client, it's a wonder that more reps aren't thrown out on their ears.

Since most buyers talk to many sales reps over the course of a day, ask yourself this question before you pick up the phone or knock on the door: What will the prospect hear from you that he probably hasn't heard from anyone else today?

A Command of the Right Questions to Ask

To build an emotional connection with your prospects, questions are the bridge on which you'll walk to get there. Tim Wackel, the sales pro we met in Chapter 2, believes that asking fantastic questions is the way that a rep's credibility is built. "You demonstrate expertise by asking questions, not talking," he says. "You become a person that people value by finding out how potential customers think, behave, and the things they believe in."

Most every dominant player in any selling environment works to master the art of asking questions. In fact, if you ask the right kinds of questions in the right sequence, not only can you get a realistic picture of the prospect's needs, you can also simultaneously reveal to the prospect that your solution is a viable option for their situation.

Joe Gianni is president and CEO of 2Logical (www. 2logical.com), an international leadership and sales training company based in Rochester, New York. 2Logical has been retained by many of the largest and most successful category leaders in the business world. Gianni's company has developed a question sequence that allows his reps to learn all they can about their potential customers—and vice versa.

"We've perfected the asking of questions in a highly orderly fashion, so that we're finding out what we need to know about their situation, while at the same time raising their awareness of our capabilities," says Gianni.

There are dozens of books and resources that will help you create the very best customer questions possible. Read them. Absorb them. Get your hands on as many potential resources as you can. Memorize them, and then make up your own based on all that you've learned.

Answers to the Most Common Objections

The sports ticket sales reps with whom I work regularly hear a number of objections from potential ticket buyers. Depending on the situation, people may be angry or disappointed with the team's performance, the coach, the owner, the stadium, the beer prices—any number of things.

Knowing this, we can anticipate these reactions and prepare several well-worded answers to the top objections. In advance of my visit to the team's market, I'll do some research on what the fans are saying and thinking, and prepare several carefully worded answers to their top objections. Here are a few examples:

Objection: "I prefer to watch the game on my high-definition TV."

♦ I like to watch on TV, too . . . but unless you've been to a game, you don't know what you're missing!

♦ There's so much more that happens at the game when you're there that is never even shown on TV.

♦ You can see what takes place between innings, away from the play, and all the fun that goes on in the park for the fans while the commercials are on TV.

♦ The smell of the hot dogs, the fresh air and sunshine, the atmosphere all around you—you can't get *that* through your TV!

♦ Some of the most entertaining parts of the game occur when the TV audience isn't watching—things like audience contests, fan participation, giveaways, and many more things that make it fun to be at the ballpark.

♦ There's interaction all around you, people who you don't even know are high-fiving you—where else does that happen?

♦ High-def is great ... but there's nothing more high-def than being there live and in person!

Objection: "I was very disappointed in the team's play last season."

♦ We're disappointed in the way the season ended up, too ... but we're *very* optimistic about our team and what's ahead for this year.

♦ It was still exciting to be at the ballpark; no one could have predicted what happened to us last year! (*Cite examples of uncontrollable issues—injuries, close games, and so on*).

♦ On the positive side, we were able to ... (*cite positive examples—new players that came up and contributed to the team, for example*) ... And we still had plenty of excitement at the ballpark ... (*cite examples of superior individual performances, awards, and so on.*)

♦ We're not looking back—we're looking ahead!

♦ Things can turn around very quickly! Look at teams like ... (*cite examples of teams that did poorly two years ago and turned things around last season*).

♦ No one can predict what will happen in sports, which is part of what makes it exciting and fun to follow, but we're working hard to put together an exciting team for this season!

♦ All we need are a few more things to go our way.

♦ Sports is a business that goes in cycles; teams that are on the bottom do eventually rise to the top. If you wait until we're in the World Series again, it will be too late.

♦ Winning *is* important to us, but regardless of what happens on the field, we can help to make your experience at the ballpark the very best it can be.

♦ Don't miss the next great run of baseball here in town!

Objection: "We've had to cut back on expenses."

♦ We hear from plenty of companies that are cutting back, but there are several that are shifting money *away* from things that *aren't* working to those that *are*. Are there some things you're spending on now that have run their course—and that you could replace with these seats?

♦ What sorts of things have you had to cut back?

♦ We hear that a lot. Fortunately, for some people, that means there are some excellent seat locations available at a *great* value right now.

♦ So if there was an idea that could potentially make the company money in today's marketplace by using these seats effectively, you wouldn't be open to that?

♦ You're still going to need the essentials, right? Those things that *make* the company money?

♦ What if I could show you a way that other companies like yours *make* money with their seats? Would there be an opportunity for us to work together then?

♦ Are you cutting back, or reevaluating? It's a good idea for everyone to take a closer look at what they're spending every now and then and evaluate what kind of return they're getting. What do you do for things like client entertainment right now?

♦ We're finding that companies have fewer people on staff to do the same amount of work and that company morale has been an issue. What's it been like for you?

♦ Are there budgets for employee retention we could tap into? Maybe sales incentives, HR, or marketing? I have some companies that split the expense into a couple of different budget columns, depending on how they use them. Would that be an option?

The top-selling reps in sports have several excellent responses to the objections they hear most often—and can quickly find common ground with even the angriest fan.

Asking for the Business

Gaining commitment, confirming the order, closing—call it what you will, those who make a good living in sales know how to bring home a deal by asking.

Here's a list compiled from some of the very best in the business, some of whom we've already heard from in prior chapters, including Dave Gifford:

♦ So, can I lock this in for you today?
♦ So, can we count you in?
♦ So, does that sound about right to you?
♦ Are you on board with this, then?
♦ Are we a go?
♦ How does that sound?
♦ If I can guarantee this for you today, can we go ahead and put your name on it right now?
♦ So let's button this up and get you started, all right?
♦ Well, what are we waiting for? Let's get you set up with this program, okay?
♦ It sounds like it's the right plan for you. Let's go ahead and put it in, shall we?

- From all you've told me, ____, I truly believe this program is the right one for you. Shall I put it in for you?
- So if you want a program that satisfies everything we've talked about, this is it. Can we say it's a done deal?
- It sounds to me like this is what you're looking for, so why don't we lock it in for you now?
- From the others I've worked with, ____, I know from experience that this program will do what you need it to do. Let's do it and move forward, okay?
- You have it in the budget . . . I think I've answered all your questions . . . we seem to be on track . . . the only thing left is for you to say "Yes!"
- Which credit card will you be using?
- Okay, here's the deal. You're the buyer, and I'm the seller, and I'm done selling. So now it's your turn. Can we count you in as a member of the family this year? *(I credit Dave Gifford with this fun, entertaining final close.)*

Continuing to Deliver Long-Term Value

Many sales relationships are just beginning once the sale is made. Depending on the nature of your product or service, there may be several opportunities to create value for a customer over their lifetime, and indeed, the very first sale is often a tiny fraction of their overall revenue potential.

I believe that reps can become so focused on bringing in new business that they miss out on the potential opportunities realized by continuing to serve those who already have a relationship with them. That's why 800-Pound

Gorillas balance their potential new opportunities with their already established relationships, allowing for growth on both sides.

THE CUSTOMER IS ALWAYS ... THE CUSTOMER

If your selling fundamentals are solid, every now and then you should make sure that your fundamental selling message is the right one. Regardless of how big or small you are in your niche, the 800-Pound Gorillas of any industry are the ones that continually ask their customers how they're feeling about the use of their products, because those changing perceptions can fundamentally change the way they should market and sell themselves.

Perhaps no one knows this better than multinational manufacturer Procter & Gamble. P&G is a global 800-Pound Gorilla whose products are used three billion times a day around the world. You likely know most of them by name: Tide detergent, Crest toothpaste, Pampers diapers, and Olay skin care products are just a few. P&G is ranked number six on *Fortune* magazine's World's Most Admired Companies for 2009, and number two in *Chief Executive* magazine's Best Companies for Leaders.

Since the year 2000, profits at Procter & Gamble have risen by more than 300 percent. That's because in addition to focusing on their core brands, P&G is relentlessly measuring the consumer's mind-set and opinions about the use of the product itself, the measuring of that mind-set, and the adjustment of their selling messages to reflect the discovery of changing consumer tastes and attitudes.

Feminine care products, for example, come in two basic product types: sanitary napkins and tampons. Procter & Gamble commands nearly 50 percent of this $600 million-plus industry and continues to do extensive interviews and research on not only its products' performance but *why* consumers choose one *type* of product over another.

P&G research has shown that while most women alternate between pads and tampons based on the severity of their menstrual cycles, there are two different user mindsets that exist for each product, and they advertise each differently.

Patricia Perez-Ayala, vice president of the feminine care division, explained it in a 2009 *New York Times* article: "A pad mind-set is much more embracing the period and is much more accepting because it's part of being a woman. A tampon mind-set is like, 'Period'—what period? I don't even want to talk about it."

Through its research, P&G has learned that the old-fashioned images of freshness and cleanliness, like women in white chiffon in a field of daisies or riding a white horse on a beach, are passé and don't resonate with today's consumer. Instead, for the 2009 campaign, ad agency Leo Burnett USA used a more direct, tongue-in-cheek approach to the presentation of the Tampax product: a Mother Nature character delivering a "present," a box gift-wrapped in red, to unsuspecting women in different circumstances.

One ad features the red box being presented to a white bikini-clad woman sunning herself on a beach. "Mother Nature here, bringing Kate her monthly gift: her period," smiles the actress. Looking at the barely-there bikini, she says with raised eyebrows, "Good luck wearing *that* with backup," meaning wearing a pad behind a tampon on potentially heavy-flow days. Kate winks at the camera as she reaches into her beach bag and pulls out a box of Tampax Pearl tampons. The message at the end: "Outsmart Mother Nature with Tampax."

Leo Burnett's ads for P&G's Always sanitary napkins, however, are much different. Not wishing to hide the fact that periods are a fact of life, the Always brand almost celebrates it, and uses the tagline, "Have a happy period" to reinforce it.

These two campaigns speak to the same situation, yet with a very different selling message to each kind of product user, based on the mind-set of each. Through its research, P&G has learned that the idea of Mother Nature being an adversary doesn't connect as well with those who prefer pads, and the notion of a "happy period" is unthinkable to women who choose tampons. To read more about the campaign click on www.nytimes.com/2009/03/20/business/media/20adco.html.

QUICK TO PICK UP

Paper towels are a fairly boring household commodity, but they are advertised frequently to build brand awareness and to reinforce the product's positive qualities. P&G's Bounty brand is a market leader, using the "quicker-picker-upper" tagline in its ads for nearly 40 years. What they've found recently, however, is that moms aren't prone to want to be portrayed as "panicked" when little Jimmy drops the tumbler filled with orange juice any more.

What P&G has learned is that today's moms—the primary purchase decision makers—are more relaxed about household spills than they used to be. They want to feel in control, and they don't want to feel like a paper towel has to come to their rescue. They want to be perceived by others as being in charge of the situation, no matter how messy it is.

So how have their ads changed? No more panicked gasps from Mom as she watches the school volcano project erupt all over her kitchen. Bounty's new phrase for 2009—and Mom's new attitude—is "Bring It." She's calm, totally together, and has it under control. And the Bounty brand, of course, is behind her all the way.

Is it a more difficult sell in a tougher economy? Yes, and spending on this category is slightly more discretionary than some other things, meaning that if people really need paper towels, they may choose a less expensive brand. What Procter & Gamble has come to realize through its relentless surveying, however, is that the measurement of the performance of its products, as well as the perception of its brand and how people want to feel when they buy them, can converge to make a huge difference at the cash register.

You'd hate to think that you've been using the wrong selling message all along. This is why it's so important to get back to the basics frequently; to make sure that you're doing all you can to maximize every selling opportunity.

TAKEAWAYS

Master the Fundamentals

♦ **All 800-Pound Gorillas do the little things exceptionally well.** Those things that others tend to think of as unimportant are the secret weapons of those who dominate their industry.

♦ **Consistent training on the fundamentals is a necessity for any dominant player—company or individual—to continually seek out and take part** in regularly. Whether you or your company chooses to invest in it, understand that you as an individual are the one who benefits most from consistent education.

♦ **Dominant players make sure their people are constantly improving on several key sales activities.** These include:

  ♦ A thorough knowledge of the product.

  ♦ A straightforward, confident opening.

  ♦ A good, solid command of the right questions to ask.

  ♦ An understanding of the most common objections and the proper responses.

  ♦ An ability to ask for the business.

  ♦ The continual delivery of value for that customer over the long term.

♦ **The best companies look outside their own worlds regularly and make sure they know what's important to others.** Focus groups, surveys, and other tools help the most dominant players to adapt to changing behaviors, tastes, and perceptions, so that the sales fundamentals they're using can remain effective.

13

THE ACTION PLAN

How You Will Become the Next 800-Pound Gorilla

Before we begin mapping out your game plan for dominance, let's make one thing clear: Not all 800-Pound Gorillas deserve the status they've achieved.

Bernard Madoff, Allen Stanford, Stefan Wilson, Dennis Bolze, and Danny Pang are just a short list of recent investment advisors who have been accused of or convicted of bilking investors out of billions of dollars in illegal Ponzi schemes. Once considered the dominant players in the return-on-investment game, these unscrupulous villains have allegedly (or otherwise) robbed thousands of innocent investors of their life savings and squandered their money on lavish lifestyles for themselves and their families.

The problem is actually much worse than we may realize. Robert Khuzami, the U.S. Securities and Exchange

Commission enforcement director, said the SEC had actually discovered and prosecuted more than 75 individual Ponzi-related schemes between 2007 and the first part of 2009.

And dominant players' dastardly deeds are not limited to the investment world. There are plenty of others whose rise to the top is questionable. Consider the enormous fallout surrounding big players like Enron, WorldCom, Morgan Stanley, former Illinois Governor Rod Blagojevich, former Senator Ted Stevens of Alaska, former NBA referee Tim Donaghy, and the use of illegal steroids in nearly every professional sport.

It certainly does make you wonder which companies and individuals are naturally dominant, and which ones are "juiced"—as former baseball player and steroid whistle-blower Jose Canseco might say.

WORLD'S LARGEST . . . PAIN TO DEAL WITH

Up until late 2008, "Mr. Big Volume" in the U.S. automotive business was Bill Heard Enterprises—which used the term "World's Largest Chevy Dealer" to describe its 13 Chevrolet auto dealerships in Alabama, Florida, Georgia, Nevada, Tennessee, and Texas. Based in Columbus, Georgia, Bill Heard posted sales figures on his company's web site of $2.5 billion a year, and the company employed more than 3,000 people.

How it arrived at that "World's Largest" status, however, had always been suspect. Several allegations of misleading advertising, questionable business practices, and sales and service complaints had plagued the company for years.

Relentless advertising that claimed to have a certain loss leader vehicle in stock at the dealership—one at a low advertised price—was found to be untrue. In another case, a $50 million deceptive advertising lawsuit was filed against the company in 2007, stemming from a bogus recall notice that was printed and mailed to 10,000 Bill Heard customers in Georgia in an attempt to boost the service department's numbers.

Heard's dealer sales practices had also come under scrutiny. They included one angry customer whose keys to his vehicle were reportedly thrown onto the roof of the building to keep him on the lot. Another customer claimed she was locked into the dealership's parking lot to force a deal. Reports from former employees claimed that the company's Internet business development team routinely told customers with less-than-satisfactory credit they had actually been approved for no-money-down credit deals for $40,000 vehicles. Then, once they arrived at the store, they were told otherwise.

"They're well-known in this department," claimed Carol Kent, the Texas Department of Transportation's director of motor vehicle enforcement, in an interview with the *Atlanta Business Journal* in 2007. "We've always had problems with them." More than 125 consumer complaints were filed against the company in Texas alone, and tens of thousands of dollars in fines assessed.

Citing the bad economy, Bill Heard Enterprises filed for bankruptcy and closed all 13 of its stores in September of 2008. According to a company statement, its business plan was dependent upon GMAC's allowance of credit for its large inventories of vehicles. When GMAC eliminated that credit allowance, the company could no longer remain solvent.

Decide to be different from those who choose to take shortcuts, give in to temptation, and grab the quick buck. Make the decision to be able to live with yourself as a dominant player and not to live to become one at the expense of others. There's only one way to do it right—and that's by not doing others wrong.

THE GAME PLAN

So let's talk about how we're going to get you to 800-Pound Gorilla status, fair and square.

Step One

Reread each of these chapters one at a time, writing little notes in the margins in answer to these questions:

- How does this relate to me?
- What ideas am I coming up with that are uniquely mine to exploit?
- What steps could I take to make this happen in my niche?

You can do a Cliff Notes version of this step by going over the Takeaways at the end of each chapter, and writing notes in those margins.

Step Two

Take a clean notebook (or a Notepad or Word file on your computer) and begin to write out your journey:

- Why do I want to be an 800-Pound Gorilla?
- What do I see for myself as a dominant player? What benefits will accrue to me when I arrive?

♦ What changes would I like to see in my life when I become an 800-Pound Gorilla?

♦ Using the 12 Attributes, how will I begin to make my way toward that goal?

Let your mind wander freely! Think B-I-G thoughts; visualize yourself as being the very best in your field, and feel what that feels like. Believe you can; your beliefs will influence your actions, just as they have all your life up to this point in your career.

Step Three

Take action! Make yourself small action steps each day and each week that will move you closer to your goal of becoming the dominant player in your niche. Ask yourself the following questions:

♦ What can I do today (or this week) that's measurable, within my reach, and brings me closer to becoming the dominant player I'm becoming?

♦ How can I break it down into steps that are easily doable for me?

♦ Who can I ask to keep me on track and hold me accountable for taking these steps?

If you'd like to access a specially created worksheet to help you achieve your 800-Pound Gorilla of Sales status, you can download and print the free Action Sheet at www.The800PoundGorilla.com/actionsheet.htm. You'll also find several other articles, examples, and resources, all free to you as a bonus for buying and using this book.

A WORD OF WARNING

Despite all of the perks that accompany this title, becoming an 800-Pound Gorilla comes with its share of scrutiny. When you're at the top of the mountain, it's more likely that others will be trying to knock you off.

Theodore McManus, marketing genius for Cadillac in the early days of the automobile, knew this all too well. In 1915, the Cadillac Motor Car Company had earned a dominant position for high quality. It was soon discovered, however, that its 1915 Touring model had several problems. Packard, Cadillac's fiercest competitor in the luxury car market, took every advantage of this chink in Cadillac's armor to try and steal market share, with ads promoting its "better" product.

McManus's response was a simple print ad that never even mentioned the name Cadillac. It was titled "The Penalty of Leadership," and it stands among the 100 most effective pieces of advertising ever written:

> In every field of human endeavor, he that is first must perpetually live in the white light of publicity. Whether the leadership be vested in a man or in a manufactured product, emulation and envy are ever at work. In art, in literature, in music, in industry, the reward and the punishment are always the same. The reward is widespread recognition; the punishment, fierce denial and detraction.
>
> When a man's work becomes a standard for the whole world, it also becomes a target for the shafts of the envious few. If his work be mediocre, he will be left severely alone—if he achieves a masterpiece, it will set a million tongues a-wagging.

Jealousy does not protrude its forked tongue at the artist who produces a commonplace painting. Whatsoever you write, or paint, or play, or sing, or build, no one will strive to surpass or to slander you unless your work be stamped with the seal of genius.

Long, long after a great work or a good work has been done, those who are disappointed or envious, continue to cry out that it cannot be done. Spiteful little voices in the domain of art were raised against our own Whistler as a mountebank, long after the big world had acclaimed him its greatest artistic genius. Multitudes flocked to Bayreuth to worship at the musical shrine of Wagner, while the little group of those whom he had dethroned and displaced argued angrily that he was no musician at all. The little world continued to protest that Fulton could never build a steamboat, while the big world flocked to the river banks to see his boat steam by.

The leader is assailed because he is a leader, and the effort to equal him is merely added proof of that leadership. Failing to equal or to excel, the follower seeks to depreciate and to destroy—but only confirms once more the superiority of that which he strives to supplant.

There is nothing new in this. It is as old as the world and as old as human passions—envy, fear, greed, ambition, and the desire to surpass. And it all avails nothing. If the leader truly leads, he remains—the leader. Master poet, master painter, master workman, each in his turn is assailed, and each holds his laurels through the ages.

That which is good or great makes itself known, no matter how loud the clamor of denial. That which deserves to live—lives.

In 1967, Cadillac had the work reprinted in a scroll format and sent to a list of customers, one of whom was Elvis Presley. Elvis was so smitten with the piece and felt as though it was written directly about his life that he had the work framed and hung in his office. He also commissioned an artist to do a calligraphy version for his bedroom in colors to match the room's décor. The original is still said to be hanging in Elvis's office at Graceland.

If you get to 800-Pound Gorilla status, beware: Everyone else is coming after you. Only those who continually exercise the 12 Attributes will maintain their position at the top, and those who find newer, better, and more productive ways to execute them will eventually supplant them at the peak. Be sure to protect the turf you've earned by revisiting and redefining each Attribute often. Don't be afraid to reinvent yourself, if necessary.

And most important—don't forget to enjoy the ride.

EPILOGUE:
REVELATION—END OF
DAY ONE

It was still raining at 5 o'clock.

It didn't matter. After the day he had just experienced, nothing could have dampened Adam's enthusiasm for his new job.

He appeared at the front door of the downtown office tower, looked up toward the sky briefly, and ran the short distance to his parked car, his briefcase in one hand and a *Chicago Tribune* draped over his head with the other.

As he was pulling out of the lot, he saw a friendly face from the morning.

"Hey—hey!" the man shouted through the small window in the parking attendant's box. "It's Adam, right?"

Adam smiled and nodded, water coming in through his rolled-down window. "That's right, Julius. You've got a good memory."

Julius pointed to his temple through his clear plastic raincoat. "I still got it up here, young man. How was y'first day? Was I right?" He was genuinely interested.

"You were right," Adam beamed. "I'm going to love it here."

"Ha-haaaa! I knew it!" Julius cackled, slapping his knee. "Git yo'self home now, 'fore this rain washes y'away. We'll see ya tomorrow."

"See you tomorrow," Adam echoed, grinning to himself as his power window rose to meet the watertight seal and his gaze turned toward the street ahead.

It was a good day, he thought. *A very good day*. He should have been exhausted; but his mind couldn't stop thinking about all he had learned. He shook the water from his coat and hair, waited for traffic to clear, and pulled out onto the one-way street.

The traffic was thick and slow. It was a good thing Adam didn't have anywhere to be; it was going to take a while to get home. With a long wait time between lights, he decided to open his briefcase on the seat next to him to dig out the notes from the day's training. He waited for the next red light, grabbed his notebook from the top of his pile of literature, and flipped the pages back to the first few scribblings of the day.

There they were: the 12 Attributes of an 800-Pound Gorilla. Adam smiled broadly and nodded to himself in approval. He felt privileged to be holding this information, knowing that Mr. Strahan never did share them with his radio audience earlier in the day:

1. Thinking Bigger Than Anyone Else
2. Being Authentic
3. Rattling the Cage
4. Doing What Others Won't
5. Being a Hero to Those You Serve
6. Talking Less and Doing More

7. Adding Value
8. Being the One Others Quote
9. Getting Beyond Rejection
10. Knowing the Competition
11. Being Passionate
12. Mastering the Fundamentals

Not only did he know them, he knew *why* they were on the list and how Consolidated has used them to rise to the top of its game. He read through the list again, thinking about how Peter had explained each one.

The light turned green. He threw his notebook back into the open briefcase, closed the lid, and turned right onto Halsted.

He had a lot to study that night, and he couldn't wait to get started.

* * * * *

ABOUT THE AUTHOR

Bill Guertin is CEO (Chief Enthusiasm Officer) of **The 800-Pound Gorilla**, a dynamic sales improvement and consulting company whose list of blue-chip clients includes the ticket sales departments of professional sports teams from the National Basketball Association (NBA), National Hockey League (NHL), National Football League (NFL), Major League Baseball (MLB), and Major League Soccer (MLS).

He is the author of *Reality Sells: How to Bring Customers Back Again and Again by Marketing Your Genuine Story* (WBusiness Books, 2007), and the author and publisher of the *Sports Ticket Sales Newsletter*, the most widely read publication devoted specifically to the sports ticket selling industry. Bill has written dozens of articles and published works in several magazines and trade publications and is a highly sought-after speaker, educator, and workshop facilitator.

The company's definition of an 800-Pound Gorilla is *the dominant player in any marketplace whose tactics and techniques result in an unfair share of the available business.* Bill works directly with client companies in nearly every industry to help them become the dominant players in the business categories in which they compete.

If you're ready to become the 800-Pound Gorilla
in your industry, contact Bill about a personalized sales
improvement program at (815) 932-5878, or e-mail
bill@The800PoundGorilla.com. Visit Bill online at www.
The 800PoundGorilla.com for additional helpful information, and sign up for his free newsletter, *The 800-Pound
Gorilla Report.*

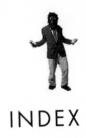

INDEX